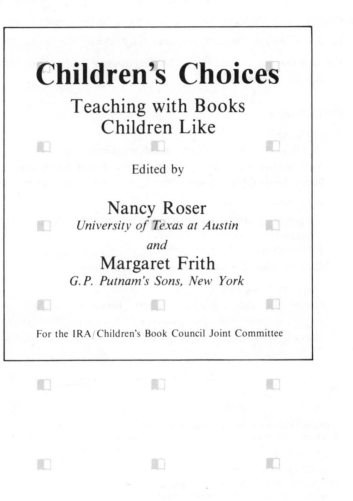

Children's Choices

Teaching with Books
Children Like

Edited by

Nancy Roser
University of Texas at Austin

and

Margaret Frith
G.P. Putnam's Sons, New York

For the IRA/Children's Book Council Joint Committee

INTERNATIONAL READING ASSOCIATION
800 Barksdale Road   Newark, DE 19711

INTERNATIONAL READING ASSOCIATION

Copyright 1983 by the
International Reading Association. Inc.

Library of Congress Cataloging in Publication Data
Main entry under title:

Children's choices.

Includes bibliographies.
1. Children—Books and reading.   2. Reading.
3. Bibliography—Best books—Children's literature.
I. Roser, Nancy.   II. Frith, Margaret.   III. Inter-
national Reading Association
Z1037.C54454   1983   011'.62   83-10697
ISBN 0-87207-735-7
Fifth Printing, July 1988

Contents

IRA/Children's Book Council Joint Committee
1980-1981

Representing IRA

Nancy Roser, *Cochair*
University of Texas at Austin

Helene Lang
University of Vermont

Mary Burns
Framingham, Massachusetts

Suzanne Curry
Wilmington, Delaware

Linnea D. Lilja
University of Missouri
  at Columbia

Helen Huus, Emerita
University of Missouri
  at Kansas City

Harold Tanyzer
Hofstra University

Bernice E. Cullinan
New York University

Representing CBC

Margaret Frith, *Cochair*
G.P. Putnam's Sons

Suzanne Coil
Avon Books

Jean Karl
Atheneum Publishers

Marcia Leonard
Willaim Morrow Company

William Morris
Harper & Row

Eleanor Nichols
McGraw-Hill

Peter Dews
Children's Book Council

Foreword

Norman Cousins, the noted author, once remarked:

> The way a book is read—which is to say, the qualities a reader brings to a book—can have as much to do with its worth as anything the author puts into it.... Anyone who can read can learn how to read deeply and thus live more fully.

As educators and individuals interested in the teaching of reading, Cousins' words paraphrase our professional mission: enabling children to live a fuller life through reading. The International Reading Association provides many services to aid us in this endeavor. One of the most valuable of these services is the annual publication, in the October issue of *The Reading Teacher*, of Children's Choices, a list of children's literature that youngsters have found most enjoyable. This list provides thousands of teachers with the raw material needed to enable children to live the fuller life mentioned by Cousins.

Children's Choices: Teaching with Books Children Like, edited by Nancy Roser and Margaret Frith, is a wonderful supplement to that annual list. In addition to providing a list of the previous Children's Choices, this book also provides suggestions for using trade books in the classroom. How can we structure our classrooms to stimulate children's love of books? Which books and poems should be selected and how should this choice be made? How can we encourage children's responses to literature? Can children be encouraged to write through literature? All of these questions and many more are answered in this book.

This volume will be a necessary addition to the professional libraries of teacher educators and classroom teachers interested in stimulating children's enjoyment of reading. As S.I. Hayakawa, noted educator and former U.S. Senator has said:

> In a very real sense, people who have read good literature have lived more than people who cannot or will not read.... It is not true that we have only one life to live; if we can read, we can live as many more lives and as many kinds of lives as we wish.

Jack Cassidy, *President*
International Reading Association
1982-1983

ABOUT THIS BOOK...

Children's Choices: Teaching Reading with Books Children Like, edited by Nancy Roser and Margaret Frith, provides suggestions for effective use of children's favorite books in the classroom—which books and poems to use, how to structure the classroom, how to encourage writing, how to stimulate children's responses to literature, and more.

This International Reading Association volume was sent to all IRA Comprehensive Members on record at the time copies came off the press. Other interested readers may order copies from IRA, Department BB, P.O. Box 8139, 800 Barksdale Road, Newark, Delaware 19714, USA.

Individual Members US$5.00 Others US$7.50

Ask also for a free copy of IRA's Publications Catalog which describes all currently available titles, including many titles directed to the classroom teacher.

IRA DIRECTOR OF PUBLICATIONS   Jennifer A. Stevenson

IRA PUBLICATIONS COMMITTEE 1986-1987   James E. Flood, San Diego State University, *Chair* • James F. Baumann, Purdue University • Janet R. Binkley, IRA • Rudine Sims Bishop, The Ohio State University • Carl Braun, University of Calgary • Susan W. Brennan, IRA • Richard L. Carner, University of Miami • Richard C. Culyer III, Coker College • Dolores Durkin, University of Illinois • Philip Gough, University of Texas at Austin • John Micklos, IRA • Ronald W. Mitchell, IRA • Joy N. Monahan, Orange County Public Schools, Orlando, Florida • Allan R. Neilsen, Mount St. Vincent University • John J. Pikulski, University of Delaware • María Elena Rodríguez, IRA, Buenos Aires • Robert Schreiner, University of Minnesota • Jennifer A. Stevenson, IRA

Introduction

The International Reading Association/Children's Book Council Joint Committee was formed in 1969 to explore areas of cooperation between reading teachers and children's trade book publishers. The need for a list of new children's trade books compiled specifically for the classroom teacher emerged repeatedly as a concern of both educators and publishers. In an attempt to fill this need, the committee initiated the "Children's Choices" (formerly "Classroom Choices") project in 1973. The unique feature of this annual, annotated bibliography is that it consists entirely of books selected by children themselves.

Every summer a group of IRA educators preselect several hundred titles from the more than 2,500 children's trade books published yearly. They choose books representing a wide range of subjects for all K-8 grade levels. Publishers are requested to send multiple copies of these books to five teams located throughout the nation. These teams, which rotate biannually, then test the books in classrooms.

Each team is headed by a volunteer children's literature specialist and includes a number of classroom teachers. Schools representing the community as a whole are used in the study, and every team involves a minimum of 2,000 children in the testing. Thus, at least 10,000 children throughout the United States are engaged each year in selecting the books on the Children's Choices list. The children read and then vote on the books; ballots are collected to preserve their reactions. After six months of testing, ballots are tabulated and, on the basis of the children's preferences, the current Children's Choices list is determined. Children's Choices is published each year in the October issue of *The Reading Teacher*. The list is reprinted and distributed free of charge to teachers, librarians, and many others who work with children and books.

In addition to offering a compilation of books from past Children's Choices lists, this volume includes a number of informative articles which describe how students' reading experiences may be enlivened through the use of books that have proved popular with other young readers.

Janet Hickman's chapter on "Classrooms that Help Children Like Books" describes classroom environments that welcome both children and books, ensuring that they meet in exciting ways. In "Choosing Poetry," Sam Sebesta addresses children's preferences for poetry, and offers suggestions for choosing (but not abusing) poetry in classrooms.

Julie Jensen and Robin Hawkins deal with direct evidence that children can write and that they enjoy reading what other children write. The chapter serves as a reminder that when children have rich experiences, including exposure to good books, writing is a logical outgrowth.

Children's responses to literature are addressed by Patricia Cianciolo and by Lee Galda and Arlene Pillar. Cianciolo looks at children's preferences for and responses to illustrations in favorite picture books. Galda and Pillar address factors affecting readers' responses to literature and offer suggestions for encouraging responses.

Dianne Monson's suggestions for encouraging literary responses among gifted and talented children address the special needs of these children, but her suggestions are intended to be adapted for others with a wide range of ability.

Helen Huus describes development of a statewide literature program that could serve as a model for other states. Helene Lang provides well-reasoned criteria for selecting books for children. M. Jean Greenlaw categorizes books chosen for the Children's Choices list and compares them with results of other research on children's preferences.

This collection reflects the suggestions of authors noted for their contributions to reading, language, and literature. It is intended to aid its users to select and use literature for many reasons, not the least of which is that children like it.

NR
MF

The editors would like to thank Peter Dews, formerly of the Children's Book Council, and Kathleen Copeland of the University of Texas for their help in compiling this manuscript.

Classrooms that Help Children Like Books

Janet Hickman
The Ohio State University

Children's reactions to books in general, and to particular titles as well, depend on many factors beyond an individual teacher's control—children's levels of cognitive and moral development, for instance, and the kaleidoscope of past experience that results in uniquely personal preferences. Yet there are some classrooms where children's responses to literature are livelier and more positive than the average, and where their choices seem to be made with more care. Such places are not just happy ,accidents. They are carefully structured environments that reflect a teacher's commitment to literature as a natural medium for children's reading and language learning as well as a source of fun and satisfaction.

What happens in these classrooms that sets them apart? Research has taken me into three such classrooms for extended observation and has put me in touch with several others. These environments are not just alike, of course, but they do seem to have a number of characteristics in common.

Children Mirror the Teacher's Enthusiasm

Being excited about children's books is apparently contagious. Teachers who make a point of talking about their own favorites or are themselves engrossed in a new title often find their students wanting to read those same books for themselves. Other signs of personal interest may catch children, too. Some teachers are able to share autographed copies of books from their own collections or they may display book-related items such as ceramic or stuffed toy characters, or posters designed by a picture book artist. However the teacher's enthusiasm is expressed, it helps to create a setting where children know that attention to the world of books is both legitimate and desirable.

1

The Classroom Is Full of Well-selected Books

In one school where children are very much involved with literature, there is a convenient library learning center right in the middle of an open space that houses eight groups of children. Even so, the teachers make sure that there are also many books in their individual classroom collections. These come from many sources. Some belong to the teachers themselves. Some are borrowed from public libraries. Others are purchased at affordable prices from paperback book clubs or publishers' overstock book stores. While a core collection of old favorites is permanently available on the shelves, many of the borrowed titles change frequently, so that there is always something new and interesting to encourage browsing.

In the classrooms I have in mind, it is not just any old books that find their way into the collection for the sake of quantity. These books are carefully chosen, and for a variety of reasons. One teacher of a fourth and fifth grade group, for example, often includes many picture books. She chooses some like Mizumura's *If I Were a Cricket* and Foreman's *Panda's Puzzle* for the special purpose of comparing the artists' ways with watercolor; there are others, like Wagner's *The Bunyip of Berkeley's Creek*, just because they are good stories and the teacher thinks the children will enjoy them. The teacher is sensitive to children's interests and the books that will have immediate appeal; thus the presence of *Tales of a Fourth Grade Nothing* by Blume, *How to Eat Fried Worms* by Rockwell, and *The Mouse and the Motorcycle* by Cleary. The teacher also recognizes that the students need some books that will stretch their imaginations and abilities, stories of sufficient depth to bear rereading and reflection. Some of the titles chosen for this purpose are Babbitt's *Tuck Everlasting*, Cooper's *The Dark is Rising*, and Steig's *Abel's Island*. Still others, like Konigsburg's *From the Mixed-Up Files of Mrs. Basil E. Frankweiler*, are available in multiple copies so that small groups can read and discuss them.

One of the notable features of the book selection in each classroom is that, whether easy or challenging, each title bears some relationship to others in the collection. There may be books by one author or illustrator, or books that represent a genre such as folktales. Other connections may be based on a content theme such as spooky things or nature books or survival stories. Teachers approach the task of choosing books with a basic plan for the kinds of relationships that may be demonstrated and a sense of the types of responses that can be expected from the children.

Children Have Easy Access to Books

In some of the book-loving classrooms that I have visited, books are not merely accessible, they are unavoidable. The ones that get the most attention seem to be those most immediately at hand, displayed where children are likely to find them at just the right moment. Brady's *Wild Mouse*, with its sketches and journal entry format that encourages close observation of a baby animal's development, may be propped up near the gerbil's cage. Poetry and art books that contribute to a theme of "colors" might line the chalk trough, with all their attractive colors showing. Books by one author may be featured on the top surface of a low bookcase, or children's own "favorites of the day" might be arranged on the window ledge. Whatever the location or selection, the key seems to be that the books are within easy reach, and prominently displayed so as to highlight the focus for which they were chosen. Books tucked away on shelves with only their spines showing give a tidy appearance, but are less inviting to prospective readers than those which are featured by virtue of a special placement.

The easy availability of a book also seems to influence children's inclinations to talk about it. In informal interviews with children about their favorites, the writer spent considerable time waiting while the book in question was located and produced as evidence. Multiple copies of a single title being discussed by several students make it possible for each one to refer to the text for examples and questions, thereby raising the level of that discussion. In almost every circumstance, students have more to say about a story they can hold in their hands than about one they must keep in their heads.

Children Have Time to Browse and Choose and Read

Attractive book arrangements are of little value unless children have plenty of opportunity to get at them. Children need time to browse and make choices, and time to read those choices—legitimate, designated time, over and above the option of getting a book when other work is finished. In most of the classrooms that serve as reference points here, teachers schedule a daily period of silent sustained reading in which children can enjoy books of their own choosing.

Sometimes this period is not really so silent, since one child may be reading aloud to the teacher or an adult volunteer, and various pairs of children may be reading to one another here and there around the room. For some children, and especially for those who are just becoming independent readers, the chance to share reading time maintains interest and generates enthusiasm for specific books. Silverstein's *Where the Sidewalk Ends* passes from hand to hand in one group of second and third graders, with frequent stops for comparing favorites and joint efforts to read the more difficult verses. The fact that the children have this chance for reading together seems to amplify the book's natural appeal by adding the attraction of pleasant social contact.

On the other hand, for some older elementary children, literature is an intensely private experience, passionately felt, that calls for long stretches of uninterrupted time. In book loving classrooms, the teacher tries to make this kind of time available. Some intermediate grade teachers schedule independent work activities after the silent reading period so that students who become deeply involved in a story may keep reading. When Paterson's *The Great Gilly Hopkins* was first introduced in one such group, a fifth grade girl who had reached the middle of the book found that she couldn't put it down. Luckily she didn't have to; the flexible schedule allowed for her interest, and her teacher recognized the value of such periods of intent attention in the ultimate development of a reader.

Children Get Personal Introductions to Special Selections

In spite of the importance of self-selection in motivating children's reading, the teachers the writer has seen at work do not simply display books and then hope for the best. They try in various ways to make sure that appropriate books fall into the right hands. The student who was so captivated by Gilly

Hopkins might not have read the book at all if the teacher had not handed it directly to her with a comment about the title character and a request to "let me know what you think of it." Like adults, children seem to find it irresistible to have their personal opinions truly valued.

Occasionally new books may speak for themselves, but for the most part teachers treat them as guests at a party—worthy of individual introduction—in the hope that children will come to see them as friends. One primary teacher points out nearly every new addition to the classroom library, making a comment on each book and putting it in some sort of perspective tied to the children's experiences: "This is like the story we read yesterday." or "Here's another book by Anno." or "John, I thought of you right away when I saw this one." Not only do these clues intrigue potential readers, they also help children begin to build the sense of connection characteristic of mature response to literature.

The Teacher Reads Aloud Every Day

Another characteristic of classrooms where children develop positive attitudes about books is that there are opportunities to hear stories as well as to read them, and this is just as true for the upper grade levels as for kindergarten and primary groups. Reading aloud to the class serves a number of purposes. In providing common experience, especially in classrooms where small group and individualized work is the rule, reading aloud furnishes a basis for group discussion and leads to shared meanings and points of references. At any level, reading aloud to the group provides children an access to stories and poems that they could not (or would not) read for themselves. The general effect is to stimulate interest and to make books as a whole, and one particular book, seem easier and more desirable. For example, when a teacher reads aloud Baylor's *Guess Who My Favorite Person Is* (because its leisurely tone may discourage children at first) or the Colliers' *My Brother Sam is Dead* (because a clear understanding of its historical background is necessary to receive the impact of its dramatic events), some students will be eager to read these same books on their own. Students also will be more receptive to other books written by Byrd Baylor or the Collier brothers.

Many teachers use their selection of read-aloud books as a tool for nudging children into the familiar, to help increase their literary awareness, and extend the range of forms and conventions with which they feel comfortable. One teacher, who was concerned that younger fourth graders might be confused by the fantasy device of transformation in *A Stranger Came Ashore*, decided to read other shorter tales of magical changes before beginning the Hunter book. Students heard *Beauty and the Beast* in Pearce's version; Tresselt's retelling of Matsutani's *The Crane Maiden*; Perrault's *Cinderella*; and native American myths like *The Ring in the Prairie* by Schoolcraft, all of which gave them reference points for talking about the more complex story.

Although reading aloud may sometimes fill those odd moments between a completed activity and the bell, it's important to note that sharing literature is not just a "time-killer" in these successful classrooms. Its purposes are too serious and too central to the reading and language program as a whole to be treated in such an offhand way; time for reading aloud is regularly scheduled time, and long range thought and planning go into the decisions made about types of books and poems that will be presented during the year.

Books Are the Subject of Much Comment and Discussion

In classrooms where books are much in evidence, their presence engenders a considerable amount of spontaneous talk: "Oh, that's a good one." "Did you read this?" "Look at this picture!" My own personal introduction to the book *Small Worlds Close Up* by Grillone and Gennaro came from a 10 year old who wanted me to see a magnified human hair. "Boy," he said, "is it ever gross!" While this is hardly high-level critical commentary, it does reflect a natural beginning point in expressing response to literature, and an inclination toward real person-to-person conversation about books. Teachers who recognize that children nourish their interest in reading through these opportunities to offer a book to a friend, laugh together about it, give a personal opinion, maybe even argue a little, legitimize the social behavior that makes such contacts possible. Absolute silence is not necessarily a good rule for the book corner.

While comments come unsolicited when the opportunity is there, true discussions are usually the result of planning. The whole group might discuss a book which has been read aloud, or a few students might meet with the teacher to consider something they have been reading on their own, or an individual conference might be held. In any case, the most satisfying discussions seem to be those where children have a chance to say in their own way what they think and feel, but where some focus and direction are provided.

Most of the teachers in the classrooms described here use book discussions as a means for teaching their students about literature, considering this a more natural context than paper and pencil exercises. They introduce the special vocabulary for talking about books as they talk about the books. Even a relatively technical term like "transformation" can be supplied when children have the idea and need a word for it. First graders know that Leo Lionni is an "illustrator," and they may have seen enough examples of his work so that identifying it as "collage" makes sense. Older children may be specific in talking about characterization or may identify different types of narrative such as legend, fantasy, and biography.

Opportunities for Representing Literature

Books become more memorable if their content and meaning are explored and extended, not only in discussion, but in other activities as well. Representational projects that involve nonverbal as well as verbal modes seem especially suitable ways for children in the elementary school to work out their own understanding of a story. Such activities allow them to manipulate materials as well as ideas, while putting language and problem-solving skills to use.

The teachers whose rooms are noted here provide work time and appropriate space for these projects. They also see that a variety of materials are available: felt for felt stories, paper and paint for murals and pictures, cloth and textured scraps for collage, castoff paper and plastic products for construction, simple props and adult clothing for dramatic play, writing paper and felt tip pens or other writing instruments, and bookbinding material. From time to time new or unusual materials are added to renew children's interests. A supply of clay and some potter's tools helped fifth graders get more involved with Macaulay's *Castle* through modeling it; a cinderblock and a collection of grains and seeds led to a replica of the mouse's home and a seed mosaic, both based on *Mrs. Frisby and the Rats of NIMH* by O'Brien.

Teachers talk to children about work in progress to give encouragement and suggestions, and to help them stay focused on the book. This also serves as an opportunity for teachers to assess children's understanding of some of the elements and devices of literature. Questioning children who are making a game board for the sequence of action in DeJong's *Hurry Home, Candy* will show something about their ability to deal with flashbacks, for instance; and children writing their own modern version of "Jack and the Beanstalk" will demonstrate much of what they do or do not know about the fairy tale form. Whatever the children's activity, teachers who tune into the process get valuable insights regarding capabilities.

Work Is Valued, Displayed, and Shared

In one of the schools where I have been a regular visitor, reminders of the children's involvement with books are everywhere. In a third grade classroom a huge brown paper mural features a painted multicolor house and the caption, *Oh, Were They Ever Happy!* Children's drawings and their dictated stories about Mother Goose are mounted on bright construction paper on a kindergarten bulletin board. Fourth graders have made dioramas and other three-dimensional constructions of monster houses based on an assortment of books about dragons and other beasts, real and imagined. All of these have been presented and explained to other children by their creators.

Such formal sharing provides an audience for children's work and lends importance to it. Displays also create a public face for the classroom environment that emphasizes the commitment to literature. When a focus is supplied through captions, labels, or the arrangement of displays, teachers can reinforce their efforts to help children make connections and comparisons, seeing particular books in a wider perspective.

Building Appreciation through Cumulative Experiences

In classrooms, important things usually happen over a period of time. Children don't become book lovers overnight. In some groups, returning to a particular book on several occasions in a variety of ways—as a writing source, a base for drama, for rereading or more discussion—is a pattern of behavior shared by students and teachers. This repetition allows for reflection and gives children a chance to learn to like books they might otherwise dismiss. One first grade teacher shared *Say It!* by Zolotow and rated the children's response as less than enthusiastic. But the seasonal content—a walk on an autumn day—was right for the time of year, the story was tied to the class' current theme study of trees, and the teacher hoped the children would claim for their own a few of the words and language patterns used by the author. Over a period of several days, the teacher planned a number of different activities. The children went outside to play in the leaves and to talk and write about the sights and sounds and smells of the season. They painted their own watercolors of a fall day. They heard the story read aloud two more times and discussed it again. By the end of this time, the level of the children's reaction had changed. They were commenting on words like "splendiferous" and "zigzagged," and incorporating them into their own stories as well. They were noticing the illustrator's techniques and talking about their effects; one pointed out that the lines "like a ditto" up and down the tree trunk made it look "very very rough." One child assured the teacher that she "really, really, really" liked the pictures and the book—and by that time, she did.

In other instances, children may be redirected to a story first met long before to give them an opportunity to discover a layer of meaning they may have missed. A teacher of 9 and 10 year olds introduced Uri Shulevitz's *Dawn* by saying the book wasn't new to them, but they would probably enjoy it again because the illustrations and the descriptive language were both so good. In the ensuing discussion, one of the children called attention to the egglike shape of the pictures and the teacher asked if the artist might have used this shape deliberately. Another student, with considerable excitement, said that it must be "like a chick hatching. Night turns into day, and the chicken comes out of an egg...." This sort of metaphorical interpretation probably would not have been within the possible range of responses for that student a few years earlier, when the teacher had first seen it.

Individual classroom teachers can provide many opportunities for exposure to a variety of good books so that children can know them more fully and like them better. But the maximum benefits of cumulative book experience come over a period of years, as children build a frame of reference for literature and learn to feel confident as readers. In some schools it is possible for children to go from kindergarten through sixth grade surrounded by well-chosen books that are easily accessible, with teachers who read aloud every day and discuss books regularly. They have continuing opportunities to represent stories in various types of activities, to share and display these products, and to take their time.

In this nurturing environment, even those children who have some struggle with the skills of reading seem to build and keep positive attitudes toward the art of reading. They enjoy stories. They savor old favorites and welcome new possibilities. In general, they reflect the efforts of teachers who have created classrooms that help children develop and sustain a real enthusiasm for books.

Bibliography

Babbitt, Natalie. *Tuck Everlasting.* New York: Farrar, Straus & Giroux, 1975.
Baylor, Byrd. *Guess Who My Favorite Person Is.* Illustrated by Robert Andrew Parker. New York: Scribner's, 1977.
Blume, Judy. *Tales of a Fourth Grade Nothing.* Illustrated by Roy Doty. New York: E.P. Dutton, 1972.
Brady, Irene. *Wild Mouse.* New York: Scribner's, 1976.
Cleary, Beverly. *The Mouse and the Motorcycle.* Illustrated by Louis Darling. New York: Morrow, 1965.
Collier, James Lincoln, & Collier, Christopher. *My Brother Sam Is Dead.* New York: Four Winds Press, 1974.
Cooper, Susan. *The Dark Is Rising.* Illustrated by Alan Cober. New York: Antheneum, 1973.
DeJong, Meindert. *Hurry Home, Candy.* Illustrated by Maurice Sendak. New York: Harper & Row, 1953.
Foreman, Michael. *Panda's Puzzle.* New York: Bradbury Press, 1978.
Grillone, Lisa, & Gennaro, Joseph. *Small Worlds Close Up.* New York: Crown, 1978.
Hunter, Mollie. *A Stranger Came Ashore.* New York: Harper & Row, 1975.

Konigsburg, E.L. *From the Mixed-Up Files of Mrs. Basil E. Frankweiler.* New York: Atheneum, 1967.

Macaulay, David. *Castle.* Boston: Houghton Mifflin, 1977.

Matsutani, Miyoko. *The Crane Maiden.* Illustrated by Chihiro Iwasaki. English version by Alvin Tresselt. New York: Parents Magazine Press, 1968.

Mizumura, Kazue. *If I Were a Cricket.* New York: Thomas Y. Crowell, 1973.

O'Brien, Robert. *Mrs. Frisby and the Rats of NIMH.* Illustrated by Zena Bernstein. New York: Atheneum, 1971.

Paterson, Katherine. *The Great Gilly Hopkins.* New York: Thomas Y. Crowell, 1978.

Pearce, Philippa. *Beauty and the Beast.* Illustrated by Alan Barnett. New York: Thomas Y. Crowell, 1972.

Perrault, Charles. *Cinderella.* Illustrated by Errol LeCain. New York: Bradbury Press, 1973.

Rockwell, Thomas. *How to Eat Fried Worms.* Illustrated by Emily McCully. New York: F. Watts, 1973.

Schoolcraft, Henry Rowe. *The Ring in the Prairie, A Shawnee Legend.* Ed. by John Bierhorst. Illustrated by Leo and Diane Dillon. New York: Dial Press, 1970.

Shulevitz, Uri. *Dawn.* New York: Farrar, Straus & Giroux, 1974.

Silverstein, Shel. *Where the Sidewalk Ends.* New York: Harper & Row, 1974.

Spier, Peter. *Oh, Were They Ever Happy!* New York: Doubleday, 1978.

Steig, William. *Abel's Island.* New York: Farrar, Straus & Giroux, 1976.

Wagner, Jenny. *The Bunyip of Berkeley's Creek.* Illustrated by Ron Brooks. New York: Bradbury Press, 1977.

Zolotow, Charlotte. *Say It!* Illustrated by James Stevenson. New York: Greenwillow, 1980.

Writing by Children for Children

Julie M. Jensen
Robin Rue Hawkins
The University of Texas at Austin

THE CHALKBOARD
The chalkboard chuckles,
Erased things lurk behind it;
Hidden forever....[1]

SUNRISE
Showers of color
Peeking over the mountains
Bringing one more day.[3]

TURTLE
Green, crawling creature
Moving so slowly along
A walking fortress....[2]

THE SUN
The hot sun shining down
on spring flowers
blinding too many small eyes.[4]

Basho? Issa? Buson? Shiki? No, Lara Nather, Dietra Allen, Scott Jones, and Lauren Feinberg.

Who are these writers? Lara is a third grader at Highland Park School in Austin, Texas; Dietra, a fourth grader at Pleasants School in Houston, Texas; Scott, a fifth grader at Lincoln School in Mt. Vernon, Illinois; and Lauren, an eighth grader at Baldwin Harbor Junior High in Baldwin, New York.

What do they have in common? All have had their writing published.

If the current wisdom of the professional literature were evident in school language arts programs, the published prose and poetry of children would be far more prominent in writing programs today. Indeed we are told repeatedly that one of the most powerful motivators of writing by children is the opportunity to hear and read the writing of their peers. Sharing commercially published trade books is one way to demonstrate to children that prose and poetry by young authors is valued; it is concrete evidence that children cannot only write but can have that writing taken seriously; it is food for an "If they can do it, I can too" attitude.

[1] Lara Nather. The chalkboard. *Language Arts*, September 1979, 606.
[2] Dietra Allen. Turtle. *Language Arts*, September 1980, 659.
[3] Scott Jones. Sunrise. *Language Arts*, February 1979, 170.
[4] Lauren Feinberg. The sun. *Language Arts*, April 1977, 370.

Missed opportunities to share children's poetry and prose, and thereby to enhance motivation, are no less evident in reading programs. Although the language experience approach to teaching reading may be widely recognized at the elementary level, its use of the published writing of children is extremely limited. The six existing Children's Choices lists fail to cite a single juvenile tradebook of children's writing. Clearly a rich literature for classroom reading or hearing is escaping notice.

Why Are There No Child-Authored Books on Children's Choices Lists?

1. Are there too few volumes available? Given the number of juvenile trade books published annually, the proportion of titles which include children's writing is clearly miniscule. An examination of the bibliography at the end of this chapter indicates that few have been published since 1974, the year of the first Children's Choices list.

2. Do children favor prose to poetry? At best, we know that poetry written by children is more often published than is prose. Many titles are anthologies of poetry or are prose/poetry combinations compiled from specialized groups such as innercity children, workshop participants, or contest winners.

3. Does the process of selecting Children's Choices exclude titles by children? Although nearly one-fourth of the juvenile trade books published each year are tested with children, titles which include writing by children are possibly among the three-fourths eliminated prior to field testing, that is, during the early stages of the composition of the annual lists.

4. Do children like to read and hear the writing of their peers? Teachers we know who have shared children's writing with their students strongly respond "Yes." Librarians report that child-created books are among the most popular in the library (Huck, 1979). Children seem to be interested in and to enjoy what other children write.

5. Are many teachers simply unaware of the existence of commercially published trade books composed of children's work? To these teachers we offer the bibliography at the end of this chapter.

6. Is published children's writing inaccessible to teachers? A considerable body of children's writing appears each year in professional journals and in magazines for children, rather than in book form from trade publishers. For example, *Language Arts*, a journal for elementary teachers published by the National Council of Teachers of English, considers for publication any submitted form of original children's writing and its accompanying art. Teachers can learn about children's writing contained in magazines for children through bibliographies such as Copeland's (1980). She lists twelve publications (e.g., *Child Life, Ebony Jr.!, Highlights for Children, National Geographic World, Stone Soup*) to which children might turn to enjoy the writing of their peers, and includes suggestions, requirements, and addresses for teachers interested in helping children to submit their writing for publication. Whether their primary objectives relate to reading or to writing, whether the publication is a professional journal or a magazine for children, teachers will find these publications an important source of writing by children.

7. Do teachers prefer to help children to publish their writing in publications the children themselves create? Tradebooks, professional journals, and magazines for children are only three outlets for children's writing. Teachers and librarians interested in providing students with opportunities to write for classroom, school, and community audiences and to read one another's writing may also choose to publish the work themselves. The forms of the final product may be varied. Classroom and school newspapers, for example, can range widely in their sophistication, but they uniformly provide a medium for many types of writing and for motivating children to revise and edit their writing—to create writing to be read.

Book publishing also can follow many processes and result in many different kinds of products. The professional literature provides considerable guidance to teachers wishing to involve students in the process of publishing books. Surely the most cited teacher reference is *How to Make Your Own Books* (Weiss, 1974). Weiss helps readers to bind a variety of books (scrolls, free-form, accordian, flip) and to find interesting materials for cover and contents.

From Greenfeld's *Books: From Writer to Reader* (1976), children can first learn how books are born with the author's idea, and then take a guided tour through the publishing process which results in a finished volume.

D'Angelo et al. (1981) illustrate a step-by-step process which combines several bookmaking techniques and which allows elementary children to make simple books out of everyday materials.

Hennings (1978) describes the conversion of a classroom into "Pine Brook Press," for which sixth grade students wrote, illustrated, and bound original picture books that kindergarten and first graders might enjoy. Under the aegis of the Press, students also designed, wrote, and distributed filmstrips, a quarterly literary magazine, and a newspaper. Gonzales (1980) explains how to build an Author Center in a classroom. Between Ribbon-Cutting Day and the Author-of-the-Day celebration, readers can learn about the work of becoming a published author, vicariously moving through classroom areas devoted to resources for writing, writing rough drafts, editing, making book covers, binding, and illustrating.

Finally, Huck (1979) describes how to make a book, but she does so within a lengthy and compelling context of literature as a model for children's writing and as a means of inspiring varying forms of discourse—diaries, logs, letters, newspaper articles, advertisements. She writes:

> Children's writing will grow out of exciting and rich sensory experiences that bring a depth of feeling about people, places and things. Exposure to much fine literature of increasing complexity will provide children with a cafeteria of forms and examples from which they may choose models for their own writing. Creative writing does not develop in a vacuum. A child must have something that he wants to write about and then be able to select the appropriate form for his message. (p. 670)

The ties among rich experiences, good books, and writing are inescapable. The experience of writing a book is integrative. Children can be part of each step according to their level of development and the type of book to be made. The investment of teacher effort is large, so volunteers are frequently used to type or construct books in classrooms where publishing is an ongoing activity.

Child-written books often become permanent parts of classroom and school library collections. Catalogued and shelved, these books are a clear statement by adults that they value children's writing. Proud authors have had the invaluable experience of planning, writing, and editing their writing for a larger audience than just the teacher; they have the joy of both being read, and of reading children's works.

8. Are teachers unaware of the potential of child-written

reading materials in their classrooms? We believe the potential is great. But why should children's writing be a significant source of reading material for children? How is children's writing used in classrooms? The hypothetical teacher interviews which follow represent actual practice observed in classrooms.

A Classroom View of the Potential of Child-Written Reading Materials

A walk through classrooms where writing is valued reveals several shared characteristics. In each are prominently displayed attractive arrangements of children's work covering bulletin boards, walls, doors, dividers, backs of bookcases, and even window shades. Hundreds of books from several libraries—on topics from insects to dinosaurs to fantasy—cover tables and fill bookcases, racks, and children's desks.

Teacher 1 has twenty-five first graders in her class.

Interviewer: How would you describe the role of children's writing in your classroom?

Teacher 1: Children's writing becomes their own and other students' reading material. They read what they write and what other children write and so learn to read.

Interviewer: That seems impossible. Don't children have to be able to read first, before they learn to write?

Teacher 1: Not at all. I've found that most children are able to write to some degree from the first days of school. They title their artwork and record thoughts and stories from the beginning. Those who prefer not to write begin by dictating to me. After a few weeks, all but a few write at least some of their work themselves. Reluctant writers see that other children are not penalized for their invented spellings or handwriting and become more willing to write what they, themselves, have to say.

Interviewer: Doesn't this limit their reading material rather severely?

Teacher 1: Perhaps a little at first, though beginning reading programs usually include time for teaching children the alphabet, sounds, or sight words. I've found that even if we do start out a little slower than we might otherwise, the children are soon reading far more than they would in a regular program. Further, I've found that this approach has several other advantages over a more traditional approach.

First, reading materials are tailored to fit children's needs and abilities. All of the words they read are words they already know, the sentence structures used reflect their knowledge of the language, and the content is based on their own experiences. They are not limited by predetermined vocabulary presented for memorization by the teacher. They are not forced to read contrived stories which, because of their limited vocabularies, are frequently stilted and sound artificial. From the beginning, reading is linked with writing, so children learn at the outset essential concepts about print and the sound-symbol relationships of the English language. They learn that direction is important: top to bottom, left to right, front to back. They learn that letters must be formed according to certain critical criteria in order to be recognizable and read. They are permitted to experience the joy of authorship and pride in their reading ability from the beginning.

Every child can be successful, not just the lucky few who are able to memorize and recite more quickly than the others. Since the program is so individualized, children write and read as much and as quickly as they are able. No one is slowed down, no one is left behind. I think these early successes are critically important as the children develop a concept of themselves as learners. Everyone is learning, everyone can learn.

Interviewer: But how do you know what to teach?

Teacher 1: Children's writing reveals a great deal about what they know. For example, a child who spells "cat" as "kt" is attending to both beginning and ending sounds. The letters have been written in the same order they are heard. The child already knows that the sound /k/ can be written as "k," and that "t" represents the sound heard at the end of the word.

That the middle sound is also recorded and that "c" is also used to represent the sound "k" are yet to be learned. So, depending on what the child has written over a period of time, I can tell which spelling, punctuation, and handwriting skills need to be taught. Additionally, we work on more global skills like picking a topic, generating the writing, deciding what information is important to include, revising, and editing.

Interviewer: You said before that the children's writing forms the basis of your reading program, yet you allow children to use invented spellings and punctuation. Doesn't this make reading more difficult? Also, might children's writing be a poor model for other children?

Teacher 1: Children frequently must read their work to one another. They learn from each other that the way it is written affects its readability. Also, because their writing becomes the text for reading, and because it is valuable in its own right, I edit and type their writing into book form.

Interviewer: Would you describe this process?

Teacher 1: The child's work is rewritten or typed onto sheets which are folded to become the pages of a book. The pages are then sewn by machine down the middle and glued to a cloth-covered cardboard cover. Usually a child writes three or four pieces and chooses the best for publication.

Interviewer: Don't the many corrections discourage the children?

Teacher 1: No, I don't think so. I never mark their papers, nor do I expect them to produce a corrected version of their work. We work together on one or two of the most important problems, whatever they are ready to do. Then I rewrite or type their work with correct spelling and punctuation.

Interviewer: Doesn't this require a lot of time? How do you do it?

Teacher 1: Well, I think it's an extremely important thing for me to do, so I make time for it. I have found that frequently mothers or other volunteers are willing to spend some time each week doing the typing, sewing, or gluing. The children are proud of their work and take their writing seriously. They are motivated to improve their writing and encouraged by their classmates. Their enthusiastic efforts provide me with sufficient motivation to continue.

Interviewer: Is there anything else you would like to add?

Teacher 1: I think I should add that although the children's writing is the focus of our reading program, we also spend time each day sharing and reading other books. I read aloud to my class, frequently more than once each day. I also provide time each day for children to read silently, alone, or with a partner. The books they have written are usually the first off the shelves!

Teacher 2 works with third grade students. There are thirty children in the class.

Interviewer: Would you describe what role children's writing plays in your classroom?

Teacher 2: I share commercially published children's work with my class. The students share their writing with their classmates, they read their writing to other classes, and their writing is available in book form in the school library. Additionally, they contribute to the classroom newspaper which is circulated throughout the school.

Interviewer: How does all of this happen?

Teacher 2: Children write daily in my classroom. When they've worked on a piece they particularly like, we edit it together and it is either printed or typed into a book. Some of these books stay in the classroom, others are catalogued and shelved in the school library.

The newspaper is a simple one. The children write news stories, design advertisements, write advice columns—the possibilities are endless. Two students are responsible for each edition, collecting and editing the articles to be published. This responsibility rotates, so that each student may participate. When they are satisfied with the final draft, I print or type it onto ditto masters and make copies for everyone.

Interviewer: What do you think the children learn from all of this?

Teacher 2: The children realize that writing is hard work, that it doesn't just happen. They begin to look upon their first draft as a temporary stage in a longer process, rather than as a finished product. They develop a sense of audience when their writing is to be shared and read, not just to themselves or their teacher, but to the class and possibly many other students as well. They choose their words with care, they discover that what seems obvious to them may need clarification if another person is to understand what was meant. They elaborate on the skeletons of an idea, including details which make their writing clearer and more interesting. They focus on communicating ideas and experiences.

The newspaper imposes different requirements on their writing; they learn to adapt their writing style to the purpose of the writing.

When writing is to be published, children see a purpose for correct spelling and punctuation that is absent from unconnected worksheet drills. Writing which is to be read requires that such conventions be used lest the mechanics interfere with the message.

I've also noticed that children's criticism of their own and each other's work has become increasingly sophisticated. They focus on specific aspects of the piece of writing in question; they now comment that a section is unclear or uninteresting because it lacks detail, rather than saying they do or do not like something.

Children Can Write: Some Evidence

WHEN I GROW UP!
When I grow up, what shall I be,
A sailor sailing on the sea?
Or shall I be a soldier bold,
And always do as I am told?

A pilot flying in the sky,
Above the clouds away up high?
A postman who delivers mail?
A fisherman who braves each gale?

Perhaps a farmer on the land?
To be a fireman would be grand.
Or shall I drive a speedy train
In sun and snow and wind and rain?

Or shall I be an astronaut,
High up there in space?
Or a brilliant teacher,
Of the human race?

So many things I'd like to be!
To choose is very hard, you see.
I must choose one from all the rest,
And I will choose the very best!

> Alexi Ditter
> Age 10
> Anwatin Middle School
> Minneapolis, Minnesota
> (*Language Arts*, January
> 1980, p. 58)

Jensen and Hawkins

I TOLD MY WISHES...
I told my wishes to a tree.
I don't know if it listened,
It might have
To whisper them to others
Through the blowing wind.

I told my wishes to a bush.
I don't know if it listened,
It might have
To tell them to others
Through its small, green leaves.

I told my wishes to an ant.
I don't know if it listened,
It might have
To breathe them to others
Through its tiny feelers.

I told my wishes to a butterfly.
I don't know if it listened,
It might have
To carry them to others.
Through its gauzy wings.

I told my wishes to myself.
I know I listened,
I do that.
But I'll keep them to myself
In my heart.

> Sarah Hester
> Grade 4
> Wahl-Coates School
> Greenville, North Carolina
> (*Language Arts*, September
> 1977, p. 679)

SOUNDS

A sound may be round
like the bouncing sound
of a rubber ball
as it hits the ground.

A sound may be small
like the creepy crawl
of a caterpillar
along the wall.

A sound may be light
like the whisper of white
as snowflakes fall
in the dark of night.

Or a sound may be still
like the waiting until
a bird takes a seed
from your window sill.

> Raney Wells
> Grade Six
> Roosevelt School
> Houston, Texas
> (*Language Arts*, October
>   1980, p. 772)

THE EASTER SURPRISE

Once there was a rather unusual rabbit. This particular
rabbit hated carrots. All of his brothers and sisters knew about
it, too. While everyone else was feasting on carrots, he would eat
corn. One day his mother asked him, "Why don't you eat
carrots?"

He said, "I hate carrots."

His mother said. "Why don't you try them?" So he did.

"Hmmm, I like them." And that was the Easter surprise.

> David Jackson
> Grade 2
> Condit School
> Houston, Texas
> (*Language Arts*, April 1980, p. 445)

THE CAT'S VIEW

A gentle cat
Twitches its eye
To see the golden moon pass by,
To see a nest of birds be born,
To see space,
The cloak the moon has worn.

Robert R. Walter
Age 10
Port Tobacco Elementary School
Port Tobacco, Maryland
(*Language Arts*, September
1980, p. 620)

THE ARGUMENT

The wind roars with excitement!
Thunder clamors in anger!
The trees draw toward each other.
The sky is dark and evil gray.
Rain strikes the window....
They settled the argument now.

Jackie Stultz
Grade 5
Lincoln School
Mt. Vernon, Illinois
(*Language Arts*, March
1979, p. 250)

Whenever I want to talk,
But no one wants to listen,
Whenever I'm feeling low,
And there's no one there to lift me,
Whenever I want some love,
And no one's there to give it,
Whenever I'm confused,
Whenever I'm hurt,
Whenever I need understanding,
Or when I just want a friend,
　　　　I write.
For a paper and pencil won't argue,
And they won't disagree.
They'll just wait and listen,
To whatever is being created through them.
It's funny how such a small thing
Can bring such comfort....
　　　　Writing.

> Rosie Orlando
> Age 13
> Kane Senior Public School
> Toronto, Ontario, Canada
> (*Language Arts*, October
>   1980, p. 755)

Bibliography of Trade Books
Containing Prose and Poetry by Children

Allen, T.D. (Ed.). *Arrows Four: Prose and Poetry by Young American Indians*. New York: Washington Square Press Pocket Books, 1974.

Baldwin, Michael. *Poems by Children*. London: Routledge & Kegan Paul, 1962.

Barnstone, Aliki. *The Real Tin Flower: Poems about the World at Nine*. New York: Crowell-Collier, 1968.

Baron, Virginia Olsen (Ed.). *Here I Am! An Anthology of Poems Written by Young People in Some of America's Minority Groups*. New York: E.P. Dutton, 1969.

Benig, Irving (Ed.). *The Children: Poems and Prose from Bedford-Stuyvesant*. New York: Grove Press, 1971.

Berger, Josef, & Berger, Dorothy. *Small Voices*. New York: Paul S. Erickson, 1966.

Birmingham, John (Ed.). *Our Time Is Now*. New York: Frederick A. Praeger, 1970.

Conkling, Hilda. *Poems By a Little Girl*. London and Sydney: George G. Harrap, 1920. New York: Frederick A. Stokes, 1920.

Cornish, Sam, & Dixon, Lucian W. (Eds.). *Chickory: Young Voices from the Black Ghetto*. New York: Association Press, 1969.

Divoky, Diane (Ed.). *How Old Will You Be in 1984?* New York: Avon Books, 1969.

Dorothy. *How the World Began*. New York: Pantheon, 1964.

Dunning, Stephen (Ed.). *Mad, Sad, and Glad*. New York: Scholastic, 1970.

Duva, Nicholas (Ed.). *Somebody Real: Voices of City Children*. Rockaway, New Jersey: American Faculty Press, 1972.

Ford, Boris. *Young Writers-Young Readers*. Tarrytown, New York: Hutchinson, 1963.

Graham Educational Products (formerly Fun Publishing Company). *Anthologies of Writings By Children*. Indianapolis: Graham Educational Products, varying dates.

Grossman, Barney, Groom, Gladys, & Pupils of the P.S. 150, The Bronx, New York. *Black Means....* New York: Hill & Wang, 1970.

Holland, John (Ed.). *The Way It Is*. New York: Harcourt Brace Jovanovich, 1969.

Hopkins, Lee Bennett (Comp.). *City Talk*. New York: Alfred A. Knopf, 1970.

Jordan, June, & Bush, Terri (Comps.). *The Voice of the Children*. New York: Holt, Rinehart and Winston, 1970.

Joseph, Stephen M. (Ed.). *The Me Nobody Knows: Children's Voices from the Ghetto*. New York: Avon Books, 1969.

Koch, Kenneth. *Rose, Where Did You Get That Red?* New York: Random House, 1973.

Koch, Kenneth. *Wishes, Lies, and Dreams*. New York: Random House, 1970.

Kohl, Herbert, & Cruz, Victor Hernandez (Eds.). *Stuff: A Collection of Poems, Visions, and Imaginative Happenings from Young Writers in Schools—Open and Closed*. New York: World Publishing, 1970.

Larrick, Nancy (Ed.). *Green Is Like a Meadow of Grass: An Anthology of Children's Pleasure in Poetry*. Champaign, Ill.: Garrard, 1968.

Larrick, Nancy (Comp.). *I Heard a Scream in the Street: Poems by Young People in the City*. New York: M. Evans, 1970.

Larrick, Nancy (Ed.). *Somebody Turned on a Tap in These Kids*. New York: Delacorte, 1971.

Lewis, Richard (Comp.). *Miracles: Poems by Children of the English Speaking World*. New York: Simon & Schuster, 1966.

Lewis, Richard (Comp.). *The Wind and the Rain: Children's Poems*. New York: Simon & Schuster, 1968.

Lewis, Richard (Comp.). *Journeys: Prose by Children of the English Speaking World*. New York: Simon & Schuster, 1969.

Lewis, Richard. *There Are Two Lives: Poems by Children of Japan*. New York: Simon & Schuster, 1970.

Lonette, Marisa. *One Day Means a Lot*. New York: Bobbs-Merrill, 1965.

Mendoza, George (Comp.). *The World from My Window*. New York: Hawthorn Books, 1969.

Mirthes, Caroline, & Children of P.S. 15. *Can't You Hear Me Talking to You*. New York: Bantam, 1971.

Pellowski, Anne, Sattley, Helen, & Arkhurst, Joyce (Comps.). *Have You Seen a Comet? Children's Art and Writing from Around the World*. New York: John Day Company, 1971.

Prague. *I Never Saw Another Butterfly*. New York: McGraw-Hill, 1964.

Rosenbaum, Robert A. (Ed.). *Growing Up in America*. Garden City, New York: Doubleday, 1969.

Schaefer, Charles E. & Mellor, Kathleen C. (Collectors). *Young Voices*. New York: Bruce Publishing, 1971.

Schoolboys of Barbiana. *Letter to a Teacher*. New York: Random House, 1970.

Summers, Andrew (Presenter). *Me the Flunkie*. New York: Fawcett World Library, 1970.

Teachers and Writers Collaborative. *Five Tales of Adventure*. New York: Teachers and Writers Collaborative, 1975.

Teachers and Writers Collaborative. *Spicy Meatball.* New York: Teachers and
Writers Collaborative, published annually.

Vogel, Ray. *The Other City.* Port Washington, New York: David White, 1969.

Weiner, Florence (Ed). *Peace Is You and Me: Children's Writings and Paintings
on Love and Peace.* New York: Avon, 1971.

References

CBC/IRA Joint Committee. "Classroom Choices: Children's Trade Books 1974,"
Reading Teacher, 1975, *29,* 122-132.

CBC/IRA Joint Committee. "Classroom Choices: Children's Trade Books 1975,"
Reading Teacher, 1976, *30,* 50-63.

CBC/IRA Joint Committee. "Classroom Choices for 1977: Books Chosen by
Children," *Reading Teacher,* 1977, *31,* 6-23.

CBC/IRA Joint Committee. "Classroom Choices for 1978: Books Chosen by
Children," *Reading Teacher,* 1978, *32,* 28-46.

CBC/IRA Joint Committee. "Children's Choices for 1979," *Reading Teacher,*
1979, *33,* 33-52.

CBC/IRA Joint Committee. "Children's Choices for 1980," *Reading Teacher,*
1980, *34,* 37-56.

Copeland, Kathleen. "Share Your Students: Where and How to Publish Children's Work," *Language Arts,* 1980, *57,* 635-638.

Day, Robert, & Weaver, Gail Cohen (Eds.). *Creative Writing in the Classroom:
An Annotated Bibliography of Selected Resources (K-12).* Urbana,
Illinois: ERIC/RCS and NCTE, 1978, 101-106.

Gonzales, Dolores G. "An Author Center for Children," *Language Arts,* 1980,
57, 280-284.

Greenfeld, Howard. *Books: From Writer to Reader.* New York: Crown, 1976.

Hennings, Dorothy Grant. *Communication in Action: Dynamic Teaching of
the Language Arts.* Chicago: Rand McNally, 1978, 272-274.

Huck, Charlotte S. *Children's Literature in the Elementary School,* Third Edition, updated. New York: Holt, Rinehart & Winston, 1979, 670-684.

Weiss, Harvey. *How to Make Your Own Books.* New York: Crowell, 1974.

A Look at the Illustrations in Children's Favorite Picture Books

Patricia J. Cianciolo
Michigan State University

Children tend to declare particular books as their "favorites" on the basis of how much pleasure and enjoyment they get from the stories and illustrations. Responses to these books usually focus on the feelings, sensations, and sensory images children experience when they read the stories and look at the illustrations. In other words, children tend to base their choices of literature on aesthetic values. Only on rare occasions do children seem to be consciously aware of or concerned about the artistic values embodied in the books they read. Rarely do children refer precisely, or vaguely, even in the most simplistic terms, to the artistic values of the texts or the graphics in the books they like. Rarely do children elaborate on how these artistic elements might affect their responses to a selection, how the artistic elements determine the extent to which they experience pleasure and enjoyment from a literary selection.

None of this is to suggest that elementary school children do not identify quality literature among their favorite books when given a chance to do so. Examination of the books included in Children's Choices over the years will demonstrate that children not only can but do select quality literature. Nor is one to conclude that children are incapable of recognizing and evaluating literary selections in terms of artistic elements inherent in quality literature (and this includes quality picture books). Indeed, numerous studies clearly demonstrate that elementary school children are quite capable of evaluating literary selections according to specific literary and graphic values—the artistic values that are inherent in any literary work of art, including picture books—when they have the benefit of direct instruction and guided experiences.

Examination of illustrations in the picture books included in Children's Choices tells us what the children's preferences *are*, not what their preferences *could be* if intervention were to occur by means of direct instruction and guided experiences. The information about children's preferences that we get from Children's Choices can be used to help book selectors start with books children will likely enjoy. Once children realize they can experience pleasure and enjoyment from literature, we can teach them how to be more evaluative and discriminating in their selections. We can help children learn more about literature as a form of art, help them take a more objective stance, and evaluate the literature they read according to specific artistic elements contained in the text and in the illustrations. Then they will be more aware that it is the artistic elements which ultimately influence the aesthetic values in literature (including, of course, picture books).

Children's Responses to Illustrations in Picture Books

In selecting picture books that children are likely to enjoy, keep in mind that there are major factors about the children themselves, and about the illustrations per se, which affect children's responses.

There are at least four variables that influence each child's perception and reception of illustrations: the child's maturity at a given age, the way in which the child is prepared for the experience of meeting the illustration, the child's emotional state of readiness overall and at the particular moment in question, and the number of times the child returns to the picture. Each teacher, librarian, or parent will have to be aware of these subjective factors accommodating them in the best possible ways using knowledge, theory of child growth and development, and experiences with children.

There are at least three major factors about book illustrations per se that influence children's preferences. The first factor is the *content* (topic or subject) depicted. The second factor is the *physical makeup* of the illustrations—color or black-and-white. If the illustrations are in color, children may have color preferences or they may be influenced by the intensity of the colors. If the illustrations are in black-and-white, children may prefer line drawings, silhouettes, or monochromatic paintings. The third factor is the *style of art* (the shape of the content) used by the artist to create the illustration. Teachers who are knowledgeable about available books will make selections that are well-received by children.

Content and Genre of Picture Books

All of the literary genres are available in picture book form—modern realistic fiction (here-and-now stories), fantasy, folktales, biography, historical fiction, poetry, and factual books. All of these genre have been included among the Children's Choices over the years, although the here-and-now stories and fantasies of all kinds—especially animal (the "ourselves-in-fur" type) and eerie creature and monster type fantasies—are most frequently designated as favorites. Humorous stories which contain gross exaggerations, slapstick, and comeuppance are prevalent in the lists each year.

The modern realistic stories chosen are usually those that focus on universal concerns and feelings of children, their families, and friends—concerns that pertain to responses they themselves or their immediate family or friends would make to circumstances or incidents occurring in their immediate worlds. Typical of the stories about children's here-and-now world are *The Accident* and *The Foundling*, written by Carol Carrick and illustrated with realistic watercolor paintings by Donald Carrick. These believable, sensitive stories are part of a series about a young boy named Christopher. When reading *The Accident*, children are likely to identify with Christopher's grief when his pet dog, Bodger, is hit by a truck and killed. When reading *The Foundling*, they may share Christopher's feeling of loyalty to Bodger's memory and his growing attachment to Ben, a stray puppy abandoned by people who vacationed at this seacoast village the previous summer.

The realities often experienced by babysitters are humorously portrayed in *George, the Babysitter* written and illustrated by Shirley Hughes. This credible account of the things that happened during the course of one afternoon, when a teenage boy took care of a family of three small children while their mother was at work, is illustrated with marvelously detailed, action-filled, realistic paintings in full color. Originally published in England under the title *Helpers*, it was a runner-up for the 1976 Kate Greenaway Medal, an award given by the British Library Association to the most distinguished work in the illustration of children's books, and the Other Award, an alternative children's book award for nonbiased books of literary merit, given by the Children's Rights Workshop in England.

Typical of the kind of humor chosen by children over the years are the slapstick and exaggerated antics one finds in *Hiccup* and *Oops*, almost wordless books by Mercer Mayer. Illustrated with black-and-white, cartoon-styled, crosshatch pen-and-ink sketches, the humor lies in the disasters that beset Ms. Hippo and her companion Mr. Hippo. In *Hiccup*, the theme is turnabout is fair play. Mr. Hippo tries to cure Ms. Hippo of the hiccups and causes her to have several mighty uncomfortable experiences. Just as her hiccups ceased, Mr. Hippo starts to hiccup and then Ms. Hippo takes her turn at delivering the same kinds of brutal cures Mr. Hippo tried on her. In *Oops*, Ms. Hippo causes one disastrous event after another—she drives her car into a stop sign, upsets a bin of oranges when she pulls one out from the bottom of a rack, breaks crystal as she clumsily saunters through a china shop, and destroys a display in a museum when she attempts to kill a fly.

Very similar to Mayer's outrageous slapstick is *The Bear and the Fly*, a wordless book by Paula Winter. Realistic pictures in full color detail the series of events that occur when a fly interrupts a family of three bears during their dinner. Not only are Mama Bear, Baby Bear, and the pet dog knocked unconscious by Father Bear in his attempt to kill the fly, but Father Bear falls off a chair and is knocked out, the house is left in total disarray, and the fly flits off totally untouched.

Mind boggling and refreshing foolishness is found in Steven Kellogg's marvelous fantasy, *The Mysterious Tadpole*. This picture storybook is about the gift of a tadpole—that grows into a gargantuan but friendly monster—from Uncle McAllister in Loch Ness, Scotland, to his nephew, Louis. With line and watercolor wash pictures in cartoon-like style, the artist fills the illustrations with a fascinating array of detailed action focusing on the antics of the tadpole, Alphonse. The story ends with Uncle McAllister arriving with another birthday present for Louis. This gift is a huge egg and shortly after it arrives at Louis' home, an unusual bird with a huge broad beak and long legs is hatched from it. The ending encourages children to speculate and create all kinds of wonderfully wild imaginings involving Louis and the new addition to his nature collection.

A marvelously satirical selection was chosen by the children when they designated *The Quicksand Book* by Tomie de Paola as one of their favorite picture books. The text in this story of comeuppance is easy to read; contains a wealth of information about quicksand; and is illustrated with full color, line and water color wash, cartoon-styled drawings. While Jungle Girl slowly sinks deeper in the quicksand, Jungle Boy lectures her about the physical characteristics of quicksand, tells her what happens to animals if they happen to wander into it, and lists a few safety rules one should follow if one falls into the quicksand. He chides her for her carelessness and dramatizes his points with charts, posters, and tables. All this time Jungle Girl (and the readers of this marvelous satirical tale) can barely contain their exasperation and annoyance with this overbearing pseudointellectual. Eventually, Jungle Boy rescues Jungle Girl from her plight, but he slips and falls into the quicksand himself. Despite his plea for help and apparent distress, Jungle Girl reminds him about the tips he gave her and promises to help him out *after* she has finished her tea. De Paola's illustrations include a subplot involving a monkey, but this is not mentioned at all in the text; observant viewers of visuals are intrigued and humored by this additional story element. The directions for making quicksand are a fine bonus to this fact-filled and humorous picture storybook.

Makeup of the Illustrations

The majority of books included in Children's Choices over the years contain colorful illustrations. This is not to say that black-and-white illustrations or even line drawings and silhouettes are rejected by children; there are some of these among their choices, too. Apparently the subject or topics of the illustrations and the shape of the content are the crucial factors that influence children's responses to picture books. In the present period of economic stress, it is especially important for book artists and publishers to think carefully before deciding whether it is really necessary to use color or whether it might be more advantageous to use all black-and-white illustrations or to alternate pages with colored and with black-and-white pictures. Spier's *Oh, Were They Ever Happy!* is in full color, and I am certain this wild tale about three children's efforts to paint the exterior of their house while their parents were away for the day would not have been the success it was with young readers if the illustrations were in black-and-white. On the other hand, the black-and-white, pen-and-ink drawings Schoenherr created for *The Wounded Wolf* by Jean C. George seem to convey perfectly the Alaskan scene. In fact, colored illustrations would probably detract from this tense and fascinating account of what happened when a wolf, gravely wounded by a caribou and too weak to keep up with his pack, had to remain on the Toklat Ridge in the driving wind and snow while the many animals surrounding him waited for him to die.

One important function of an illustration in a picture book is to provide the reader with more details about the setting, action, and characters than about the text. Furthermore, each time one looks at a picture one should be able to see more and/or become more deeply involved in the story. This task of extending and enriching the reader's response each time one looks at the illustrations is the ultimate criterion for determining the quality of a book illustration, and it is one which is found in truly distinguished picture books. Included among the Children's Choices are a number of picture books containing illustrations that meet this important criterion. The 1979 Caldecott Medal book *The Girl Who Loved Wild Horses*, written and illustrated by Paul Gobel, contains brilliantly conceived paintings. Crisp, clear, representational pictures offer the reader an immeasurable amount of accurate details about the Plains Indians: their clothing; the rituals and techniques they followed when hunting buffalo; the religious symbols used in the designs woven in their clothing and included in their jewelry and teepees; and the varieties of flowers, trees, animals, and insects found in the prairie country inhabited by the Plains Indians. All of this and more about the action and the characters in this story are provided the reader by way of the illustrations. In addition, Gobel's graphics are excellently designed in terms of balance and contrast.

The black-and-white representational sketches created by Isadora for *Max*, a story she also wrote, are filled with a wealth of details that highlight the atmosphere in a dancing class. The illustrations in *Max* capture the exuberance of youth. They inform the young reader in a comical but thorough way that training for ballet is grinding hard work. They show the variety of poses one uses in ballet, but they also show that not all ballet students can execute them as gracefully and elegantly, as perfectly and nimbly, as they should. The readers of this fine little picture book, like Max the protagonist, will be helped to view ballet as a way of life that calls for self-discipline, a satisfying and expressive form of art, and a fine way to limber up for playing baseball.

Shape and Content in Illustrations

The illustrations in the books included in Children's Choices are done in art styles that range from the realistic (representational) to the fairly abstract. Books that are illustrated in the realistic or representational art style and the cartoon style are most frequently identified as favorites, but books illustrated in other art styles are included also. The art styles used in the books included in Children's Choices range from the realistic to the sophisticated expressionistic and naive art styles, from the elegant impressionistic to the cartoon style and the photographic. Books illustrated with photographs are the least prevalent among the choices, and these books are informational and concept books. None of the choices are illustrated in the surrealistic art style. This may be due largely to the fact that books illustrated in these art styles were the least plentiful among those from which the children had to choose in the first place, for proportionately, of all the children's books published each year, few books are illustrated with photographs or in the surrealistic art style.

One can best appreciate the beautiful diversity in art styles used in the picture books included in Children's Choices by examining some specific selections in which the characteristics inherent in each style of art are demonstrated.

The exactness and beauty, the controlled gracefulness and balance of line and shape in the realistic illustrations Ingraham created with grease pencil and watercolor wash for

Calhoun's well written story *Cross-Country Cat* make this picture book an accomplishment worthy of note. The soft textures and fresh colors, as well as the action-filled pictures, should help children remember this story of how a plucky, hind-leg walking Siamese cat named Henry made his way to his home on cross-country skis when his owners inadvertently left him behind at their mountain cabin.

In contrast to the realistic illustrations in *Cross-Country Cat*, consider the illustrations in Burningham's *Come Away from the Water, Shirley* and those done by Charlip and Maraslis for Yolen's *The Seeing Stick*. Burningham used different media to depict the two worlds that Shirley lived in. For the pictures depicting her real world, Burningham used grease pencil and pen-and-ink; for the pictures depicting Shirley's more exciting make-believe world, he used full color gouache wash in addition to grease pencil and pen-and-ink. All of the illustrations in *Come Away from the Water, Shirley* are in the expressionistic art style. They seem to be undisciplined sketches suggesting only the essential structural qualities of the people and objects that are the subject of Shirley's real world and her make-believe world.

The crayon and soft pencil drawings in *The Seeing Stick* are in the naive art style. They depict with marvelous sensitivity how an elderly traveler dressed in tattered clothes teaches a blind and unhappy princess to see with her fingers, mind, and heart, and they add details about the oriental setting and culture not mentioned in the text. All of this is accomplished by means of figures which appear to be childlike in terms of artistic elements of proportion, perspective, and shape. There is a noticeable vitality and spontaneity about the naive-styled drawings by Charlip and Maraslis, and there is a simplification and awkwardness about the shapes—an apparent disregard for anatomy and proportion and perspective one usually finds in drawings by those lacking in technical skill, and commonly found in paintings and drawings by those associated with the naive artist.

Parker's impressionistic watercolor paintings that appear in Baylor's *Guess Who My Favorite Person Is?* are perfect for this concept book which alerts young readers to the beauty around them and emphasizes that one's response to life is

Cianciolo

subjective. Parker's paintings reflect a personal and spontaneous vision of reality, the notion of capturing with brush and paint, with a stroke of color and a combination of hues, an individual's perception of the moment. The result is a series of visual delights.

The cartoon-styled drawings so readily identifiable as those done by de Paola are found in *Helga's Dowry: A Troll Story*, an original tale about a troll who must marry or else wander the earth forever. De Paola's illustrations, done with ink and full color wash, are wonderfully humorous and expressive. He provokes gales of laughter by grossly exaggerating the features as well as the contours, proportions, and perspectives of people, animals, and objects.

Most of the books illustrated with photographs are in black-and-white rather than in color. The photographs in Krementz's *A Very Young Gymnast* and *A Very Young Rider* are especially noteworthy. All of the subjects in Krementz's black-and-white photographs put forth substantial amounts of knowledge; concepts and attitudes are in sharp focus. The pictures are uncluttered and precise, and the actions they illustrate are easily identifiable.

Conclusions

In the purpose of identifying Children's Choices, numerous and varied selections are made available to children from all areas of the United States. This proliferation of genres and literary selections makes it possible for children to designate their favorites from a nourishing environment—an environment that gives them a chance to exercise and satisfy their aesthetic appetites and aptitudes. Graphics art or literary critics might identify titles among the Children's Choices lists that are illustrated (and written) at rather mediocre levels, but there are any number of selections among the chosen picture books that exhibit high quality and, at times, even distinguished levels of artistic accomplishments. These are the books I focused on in this discussion of the illustrations in children's favorite picture books.

Children's comments about the illustrations tend to focus on the content of the pictures. They might comment about the color or lack of color in the pictures. Most often, children state forthrightly that they do or do not like the pictures, but seldom do their comments reveal much awareness and/or knowledge about the artistic values of the illustrations. It is an exception for a child to discuss the illustrations in stylistic terms or make any reference to the formal properties of art such as complexity, balance, or composition.

There is a substantial amount of research which demonstrates that elementary school children can be educated to higher levels of artistic awareness *and* artistic discrimination. Children can acquire knowledge about and an appreciation for different art forms, art media, and styles of art. Research also demonstrates that children can be taught to use specific criteria to evaluate art (including book art) when they are given direct instruction about these criteria and when the content and subjects depicted in these artistic forms (such as illustrations in picture books) are interesting. Professional references and dissertations abound in which such research is reported and in which particular teaching strategies are discussed. Those that are most up-to-date and comprehensive are available in such publications as *Responses to Children's Literature* (Fox & Hammond, 1980) and *Illustrations in Children's Books* (Cianciolo, 1976).

The notion is untrue that one need not be taught to appreciate, discriminate, and evaluate the beautiful in books because everyone naturally loves the beautiful. It is true, however, that all artistic appreciation does involve some degree of adventure, of working out through comparing and contrasting the beautiful, the mediocre and the inferior, and of finding one's own idea of the beautiful. Children need a chance for self exploration and discovery, and this is what the procedures amount to that are used to arrive at the titles in Children's Choices. Let us use what information this provides and move on so that children will evaluate these and other picture books more consciously in terms of their beauty, importance, and meaning.

By expanding on and applying to picture books the thesis discussed in *Teaching the Art of Literature* (Miller, 1980) and *The Literary Work of Art* (Ingarden, 1973), I can conclude this discussion on children's responses to illustrations in picture books with the following comments: There is no denying that one's response to the illustrations in picture books is a subjective experience, an experience that derives some of its character from the individual child who looks at the pictures within the context of the text. Without the subjective element there would be none of the vibrance, enthusiasm, and interest that characterizes a large portion of any aesthetic experience. Nonetheless, discriminating and critical reading of picture books (and all literature, for that matter) involves seeing the literary selection as an object that is apart from oneself. This objective part of the literary experience calls for a rational and detached stance and is determined by the work's form and by our knowledge of the characteristics which give it specific form or genre. Children should be informed about the mixed nature of literary experience, the combination of the subjective and objective. Their discussions about the picture books or any literary work should include both of these elements. Such discussions will help children appreciate that there is a broad range of possible responses brought to any one picture book, and this diversity of response is not only desirable but is a wholesome way of viewing responses to all forms of art.

Bibliography

Baylor, Byrd. *Guess Who My Favorite Person Is?* Illustrated by Robert Andrew Parker. New York: Scribner's, 1977.

Burningham, John. *Come Away from the Water, Shirley.* Illustrated by the author. New York: Thomas Y. Crowell, 1977.

Calhoun, Mary. *Cross-Country Cat.* Illustrated by Erick Ingraham. New York: William R. Morrow, 1979.

Carrick, Carol. *The Accident.* Illustrated by Donald Carrick. New York: Clarion/Seabury Press, 1976.

Carrick, Carol. *The Foundling.* Illustrated by Donald Carrick. New York: Clarion/Seabury Press, 1977.

De Paola, Tomie. *Helga's Dowry: A Troll Love Story.* Illustrated by the author. New York: Harcourt Brace Jovanovich, 1977.

De Paola, Tomie. *The Quicksand Book.* Illustrated by the author. New York: Holiday House, 1977.

George, Jean Craighead. *The Wounded Wolf.* Illustrated by Joan Schoenherr. New York: Harper & Row, 1978.

Goble, Paul. *The Girl Who Loved Wild Horses.* Illustrated by the author. Scarsdale, New York: Bradbury Press, 1978.

Hughes, Shirley. *George the Babysitter.* Illustrated by the author. Englewood Cliffs, New Jersey: Prentice-Hall, 1977. (Under the title *Helpers*, published by Bodley Head, London, England, 1975.)

Isadora, Rachel. *Max*. Illustrated by the author. New York: Macmillan, 1976.
Kellogg, Steven. *The Mysterious Tadpole*. Illustrated by the author. New York: Dial Press, 1977.
Krementz, Jill. *A Very Young Gymnast*. Illustrated with photographs by the author. New York: Knopf, 1978.
Krementz, Jill. *A Very Young Rider*. Illustrated with photographs by the author. New York: Knopf, 1977.
Mayer, Mercer. *Hiccup*. Illustrated by the author. New York: Dial Press, 1976.
Mayer, Mercer. *Ooops*. Illustrated by the author. New York: Dial Press, 1977.
Spier, Peter. *Oh, Were They Ever Happy!* Illustrated by the author. New York: Doubleday, 1978.
Winter, Paula. *The Bear and the Fly*. Illustrated by the author. New York: Crown, 1976.
Yolen, Jane. *The Seeing Stick*. Illustrated by Remy Charlip and Demetra Maraslis. New York: Thomas Y. Crowell, 1977.

References

Cianciolo, Patricia J. Children's responses to illustrations in books: A review of research. *Ripples*, 1981, *6*.
Cianciolo, Patricia J. *Illustrations in children's books*. Dubuque, Iowa: William C. Brown, 1976.
Fox, Geoffrey, & Hammond, Graham (Eds.). *Responses to children's literature*. Proceedings of Fourth Symposium of the International Research Society for Children's Literature in 1978 at Exeter, England. New York: Saur Publishing, 1980.
Ingarden, Roman. *The literary work of art*. Evanston, Illinois: Northwestern University Press, 1973.
Miller, Bruce E. *Teaching the art of literature*. Urbana, Illinois: National Council of Teachers of English, 1980.

For Dreamers, Wishers, and Magic Bean Buyers Only: Encouraging Children's Responses to Literature

Lee Galda
University of Georgia
Arlene Pillar
Fordham University

Books. We read books to learn and read books for pleasure; we laugh and cry with books, travel to new places and try on new experiences with books. We want our children to know the same special joy we feel when we connect with a book. Why? Because, as poet David McCord suggests, when we "fall into books" our lives are enriched, our worlds expanded.

But what lies beyond pleasure? What is the educational importance of reading and responding to literature? To answer these questions, this chapter considers ways to extend children's responses to their books and the educational import of those responses.

Interacting with Literature

Literature is an end in itself, but it can also be a means. Children can learn to read and write through literature, extending their listening and speaking skills at the same time. By its very nature, literature calls for imaginative responses both during and after the reading of a text. Therefore, it serves to educate the imagination.

Reading and making meaning from literature is an active process of symbolization. Readers take words of the author and infuse them with meaning; the inherent work of art flowers in the interaction between reader and text (Rosenblatt, 1978). Readers actively select aspects of the text to remember and to buiid upon, filling in the gaps which are part of it (Iser, 1978). The text itself does not embody meaning; the creation of meaning comes from the reader guided by the text. This active symbolization—the making of meaning—accounts for readers' enjoyment and appreciation of the books they read. The potential for making meaning is inherent in all readers, but its development must be nurtured. With the need for active symbolization as a text is read comes the need for opportunities to respond to literature—to educate the imagination. A teacher's role is crucial for stimulating response.

How do we help our children to operate imaginatively? We must first encourage them to experience many books in pleasure-filled ways. Second, we must offer activities to extend their responses in ways which foster the growth of imagination. Teachers need to know that responding to literature begins before the first line is read and does not end when the book is closed.

Imaginative responses take many forms ranging from quiet introspection to oral discussion, writing to dance, art to drama. The forms vary according to the talents and interests of the children, the opportunities teachers provide, and the books themselves. It is important to balance the kinds of activities provided to allow children to exercise their various gifts and explore new ways to respond.

Factors Influencing Response

Since response to literature is a complex process involving the interaction of reader and text, no two responses will be exactly alike, nor will any one child's response stay the same across a variety of texts. The multitude of factors in text, child, and environment influencing response need to be considered when teachers plan for and evaluate imaginative encounters with books.

Of primary importance is the readability or "listenability" of the text. Response is limited when the text is not accessible to the reader/listener. Other text factors which influence response can be classified as either form or content.

Form ranges from the basic mode of discourse (e.g., poetry, literary prose, or informational prose) to variety in point of view or plot structure. Readers need to take different stances toward different modes of discourse (Britton, 1970). Literary prose requires a child to adopt what Coleridge called "the willing suspension of disbelief." The ability to assume different stances is acquired as children encounter different texts; it is the basis for the development of a critical perspective.

Point of view affects response; stories with first person participant narrators sometimes pull readers into a closer identification with characters than stories with omniscient narrators (Booth, 1961). When children are reading and responding to a text which compels their identification with, their "living through" the world created in the text, they may reject the text if that vicarious experience becomes too painful (Galda, 1980).

Plot structure also influences response. Stories told with flashbacks or parallel plots, for example, have a different effect from that of stories told in a straight time sequence. Indeed, young children have difficulty following complex plots. Differences among genres are important factors: fantasy elicits different responses than does realistic fiction. Fantasy must be believable only within the world the author creates between the covers of the book. Realistic fiction deals with the real world and because of this its believability is affected by the degree of its real world plausibility.

Content, too, plays a role in response, as the many studies of literary preferences indicate. Further, characterization is important: Children seem to prefer characters who reflect the social, cognitive, and moral developmental levels at which they are or toward which they are moving (Schlager, 1978).

As reader and text interact, the reader's previous experience with other texts influences response and provides a storehouse of ideas and a basis for comparison. A reader's age and sex will also influence response to literature as is clear from the many studies which indicate that preferences follow patterns which are linked to age and sex.

Cognitive development affects response in many ways. The reading and listening ability of the child interacts with the difficulty of the text. For example, children in Piaget's preoperational stage, unable to distinguish fantasy from reality, will respond to fantasy in a manner different from children in the concrete operational stage who have learned to make that distinction (Haug, 1975). Children capable of concrete operations are often reality bound, unable to envisage alternate realities, whereas children who have acquired formal operations possess the ability to accept the idea of multiple realities. This ability becomes especially important when responding to contemporary realistic fiction, since readers who cannot conceive of alternate realities may reject the text if the author's portrayal of life does not agree with their own perceptions (Galda, 1980).

Developmental level of moral judgment also affects response (Pillar, 1980). The construal of moral dilemmas in traditional fables, for example, substantiates Piagetian theory insofar as younger children respond from an egocentric reward-punishment orientation and older children from a position that considers antecedent motives and subjective criteria in making judgments. Only with maturity can children respond appropriately to the traditional intent of fables, understanding the abstract concepts they embody.

Reader personality affects responses in two ways. First, because each reader's personality is unique, each reader will respond somewhat differently to the same text (Galda, 1980; Holland, 1975; Petrosky, 1975). Since the reader is a partner with the text in the creation of a response, the variations among responses are seen as differences, not deficits. Readers are encouraged to expand responses, but the partnership of the text is never forgotten. Teachers need to encourage and appreciate individual differences, reminding students that returning to the text is a way to clarify and verify their responses. Second, since each reader's personality is unique and relatively stable, a reader will respond in a somewhat consistent manner across texts. Teachers need to be aware of this to understand the patterns of students' responses.

The reader's expectations for reading and the classroom environment also affect response. A student who is reading only because it is required will respond differently from one who is eager to read; an unhappy student will respond differently from a happy student. Students who feel they are in a safe and supportive environment will respond differently from those who feel threatened. They will voice their responses to a text only if those responses are treated with consideration and only after they are assured of the teacher's concern and acceptance. A productive environment fostering growth (emotional, attitudinal, cognitive) is one providing interesting opportunities for responding in ways attuned to children's needs and predilections. The Children's Choices bibliography aids teachers, librarians, and parents in identifying the books children like and is a fine starting point for adults who would promote literary response.

Encouraging Responses Using Children's Choices

Teachers who know children and who know their books also know there are many starting points for guiding creative responses. The countless ways, from simple dioramas and mobiles to sophisticated panel discussions and written critiques, have become our old, dependable friends. We need to expand our repertoire to include activities specifically related to particular books. This means that we have to read the books our children are reading or at least have some general knowledge of them.

In this section, we will demonstrate the way "book extenders" can help children return to the books they have read to enrich their reading. Books from *Children's Choices for 1979* and *1980* have been used in the discussion.

Is It Red? Is It Yellow? Is It Blue? by Hoban is more than its subtitle, "An adventure in color." It is an adventure in size and in shape relations, and an invitation to open one's eyes to the world around. This book can lead children to collect objects according to colors, and should guide the development of other ways to classify objects with the features under scrutiny shifting according to the system used. The book sends children out looking at their world with heightened awareness, bringing them back again with new ideas and information to add to their responses.

The repetitive structure in Lobel's *The Pancake* inspires readers to write comparable stories after her pattern, but with different characters and a different ending. The story might also produce some improvisational theater, especially on the playground where there is plenty of room to chase the pancake. The pancake's derisive chant may even appear among the jump rope regulars, as they double dutch jump through Lobel's many characters.

Children who read Sharmat's *A Big Fat Enormous Lie*, delightfully illustrated by McPhail, enjoy talking about their feelings when they tell lies. Inspired by McPhail's illustrations, they may be asked to paint or draw their feelings or create their own enormous tall tales. Children could role play the parents and create a dialogue between them when they find the cookie jar empty and then when the boy admits his lie. A dialogue between the boy and the lie is another possibility to subtly explore feelings and reactions of the characters and the readers.

Since there are two recipes at the end of de Paola's *Popcorn Book*, expect lots of popcorn popping when your children read it. To spark an intriguing search for verification, have a copy of Selsam's *Popcorn* on hand. Some of the facts in de Paola's book differ from those presented by Selsam. The former tells an Indian legend about why popcorn pops and may inspire children to write their own legends—either about popcorn popping or about some other food phenomenon such as why celery has strings. The tall popcorn tale generates interest in reading other tall tales and stimulates explorations in science and social studies.

It is easy to see why Aliki's *Mummies Made in Egypt* is a favorite for middle grade readers. Her explanations of burial rites and the steps in mummy-making are fascinating. The illustrations are meticulously detailed and could provide the impetus for further research. Some fourth grade students found the *National Geographic* publications an excellent source of information on embalming. They took a class trip to the New York Metropolitan Museum of Art's King Tut exhibition to have a firsthand look at real mummiform coffins, amulets, and ancient furniture. They were so enthusiastic that they made a life-size craft, paper-stuffed mummy, and a cardboard sarcophagus.

Another group of youngsters used puppets to recreate Erlich's retelling of Andersen's *Thumbelina*. Although their stick puppets could not approximate Jeffers' radiant painting, they were sensitive to detail and color. Thumbelina and her walnut-size bed were miniscule as compared with the toad and the wounded swallow, but she was just the right size when standing next to the king of flowers who was to become her husband. The interest generated by the puppet show resulted in demands for reading aloud other versions of Andersen's classic fairy tale.

Often children who fall in love with a book and hate to see it end are eager to write additional chapters about what might have happened had the book continued. For Adler's *The Magic of the Glits* this could be a very appealing activity. The magical creatures called Glits, invented by Jeremy to entertain Lynette (the 7 year old houseguest for whom he must babysit), could have many exciting adventures on Cape Cod. Such writing becomes more engaging when children are asked to recall the travels afield, afloat, and aloft of Norton's *Borrowers*.

The same kind of book extension is appropriate for Hurwitz's *Aldo Applesauce*. At the end of this story about shy Aldo Sossi's adjustment to the family move to New Jersey, mention is made of planting a vegetable garden when the weather gets warmer. Children might delight in writing about that project, especially since Aldo is a vegetarian. What would he plant? Aldo is also a great animal lover, and they could have him plant something for the neighborhood birds and squirrels. DeDe, Aldo's new friend, has just what he wants—a dog. Children could dramatize a scene in which Aldo tries to convince his parents to buy him one, even though they have Peabody and Poughkeepsie, two cats.

After reading Sebestyen's *Words by Heart*, children have another opportunity for acting out a favorite episode. The scripture-reading contest between Lena Sills and Winslow Starnes is a good event for classroom dramatization. How rewarding to know that literature can serve to help youngsters learn to live by heart some of the words they have come to read!

A group of fifth grade children who had delighted in Howe's "Rabbit-Tale of Mystery" decided to retell *Bunnicula* from the point of view of the alleged suspect in the title. In this hilarious tale, Harold, the family dog, narrates his adventures with Chester, the very well-read cat, after a bunny (found in a movie theater showing Dracula) is brought to the Monroe house. Chester suspects that Bunnicula is a vampire when he finds white vegetables drained dry around the kitchen. When Bunnicula tells his side of the story in the children's re-creations, things are not quite the same. This writing project led them to rewrite Beatrix Potter's *The Tale of Peter Rabbit* from Mr. McGregor's viewpoint. As a result, the children are very knowledgeable about "who" is telling the story.

The possibilities for creative book extenders are as

limitless as a creative teacher's imagination. One such professional made a "We Recommend" graffiti wall constructed from craft paper outlined with bricks. The children could write freely on it with markers, crayons, and paint to recommend books they had just finished reading. It was one of the most popular areas in the room.

Concluding Remarks

Piaget's metaphor for the child as that of a generator/ transformer has informed the position espoused for guiding experiences with literature. He means that children are active constructors of their own knowledge and beliefs. In order to best know books children must act upon them. An ever-growing body of research helps teachers understand the complex factors influencing response and how children's adaptive accommodations build to produce it. In order to maximize response, to permit children to experience literature in the richest possible way, teachers need to take into account the characteristics of children and the characteristics of their books. A love for literature is nurtured with the rewarding reading experiences children have; creative responses indicate the nature of these satisfactions.

Bibliography

Aliki. *Mummies Made in Egypt*. New York: Thomas Y. Crowell, 1979.
Adler, C. *The Magic of the Glits*. Illustrated by A. Forberg. New York: Macmillan, 1979.
Andersen, H.C. *Thumbelina*. Retold by A. Erlich. Illustrated by S. Jeffers. New York: Dial Press, 1979.
De Paola, T. *The Popcorn Book*. New York: Holiday House, 1978.
Hoban, T. *Is It Red? Is It Yellow? Is It Blue?* New York: Greenwillow, 1978.
Howe, D., & Howe, J. *Bunnicula*. New York: Atheneum, 1979.
Hurwitz, J. *Aldo Applesauce*. New York: Morrow, 1979.
Lobel, A. *The Pancake*. New York: Greenwillow, 1978.
Norton, M. *The Borrowers*. Illustrated by Beth Krush and Joe Krush. New York: Harcourt Brace Jovanovich, 1953.
Potter, B. *The Tale of Peter Rabbit*. New York: Warne, 1902.
Sebestyen, O. *Words by Heart*. New York: Atlantic-Little Brown, 1979.
Selsam, M. *Popcorn*. New York: Morrow, 1976.
Sharmat, M. *A Big Fat Enormous Lie*. Illustrated by D. McPhail. New York: E.P. Dutton, 1978.

References

Booth, W.C. *The rhetoric of fiction.* Chicago: University of Chicago Press, 1961.

Britton, J. *Language and learning.* London: Allen Lane, The Penguin Press, 1970.

Galda, S.L. Three children reading stories: Response to literature in preadolescents. Unpublished doctoral dissertation, New York University, 1980.

Haug, F.M. Young children's responses to literature, doctoral dissertation, University of Minnesota, 1974. *Dissertation Abstracts International,* 1975, *35,* 4859A. (University Microfilms No. 75-2103)

Holland, N.N. *Five readers reading.* New Haven: Yale University Press, 1975.

Iser, W. *The act of reading: A theory of aesthetic response.* Baltimore: Johns Hopkins University Press, 1978.

Petrosky, A.R. Individual and group responses of 14 and 15 year olds to short stories, novels, poems, and thematic apperception tests: Case studies based on Piagetian genetic epistemology and Freudian psychoanalytic psychology. Doctoral dissertation, State University of New York at Buffalo, 1975. *Dissertation Abstracts International,* 1975, *36,* 852A. (University Microfilms No. 75-16 956)

Pillar, A. Dimensions of the development of moral judgment as reflected in children's responses to fables. Unpublished doctoral dissertation, New York University, 1980.

Rosenblatt, L.M. *The reader, the text, the poem: The transactional theory of the literary work.* Carbondale, Illinois: Southern Illinois University Press, 1978.

Schlager, N. Predicting children's choices in literature: A developmental approach. *Children's Literature in Education,* 1978, *9,* 136-142.

Literature in Programs for Gifted and Talented Children

Dianne Monson
University of Washington

Gifted and talented children can benefit in many ways from exposure to books on the Children's Choices lists. Involving these children in projects patterned after Children's Choices is one way of enriching a reading program for gifted and talented children. Indeed, the process of selecting books that will eventually appear on locally-produced lists of favorites can add a challenging dimension to any reading program. In addition, special kinds of literary understanding can be developed through books on the Children's Choices lists. In order to consider the many possibilities for using Children's Choices in an enriched program, it is useful to look at some kinds of growth we would like to see as a result of children's experiences with literature and also to consider how some of the Children's Choices books can help to foster that growth. The chapter will deal with those topics.

Literary Response and the Characteristics of Gifted Children

As an outcome of any good reading program, we want to see that children are able to respond to what they read.[1] If those responses are to take place, it is important that children have opportunities to read many kinds of books so they may identify the genres they enjoy most and respond to them in a variety of ways. It is also important that they have available books that range from easy reading to books that are highly sophisticated. Such a range will give gifted and talented children the kinds of challenges they need to be caught up emotionally and intellectually in a book. For a reading experience to be stimulating, a transaction must take place between reader and text. When that happens, children bring experiences to the text—experiences that will influence the interpretations of what is read. Children also *take* something from the text which enriches their lives and which may add emotional or critical dimensions to future reading. This means that the text must offer something challenging to the intellectual, social, or emotional parts of gifted children.

In addition, we hope children will 1) learn to interpret what they read in the light of their world; 2) become aware of literary qualities that help to make a book enjoyable; and 3) learn to read critically, evaluating both style and content of literature. Ability to interpret may mean recognizing that the needs and fears of humans are essentially the same now as during the early days of American history, or recognizing a moral in the outcome of a character's behavior even though it is not explicitly stated. While emotional response is a priority for all children, the abilities to sense literary quality and to read critically are important at an earlier age for gifted children than for their typical agemates. Attention to appreciation of structure and style can detract from important emotional response if children are not intellectually ready for such instruction. Even with very bright children, we must be careful to maintain a balance between emotional and intellectual response. However, intellectually gifted children very early seem to seek a sense of structure in their world. They use that structure to integrate new knowledge and generate their own creative ideas. For that reason, we need to provide activities which will help these children recognize some of the basic themes and plot structures present across genres, from folk literature to realistic fiction and fantasy. Some children also will be interested in techniques authors use when they create a work of fantasy. Other children will become absorbed in the characteristics that mark realistic fiction of quality. All deserve exposure to fine stylistic models which may inspire children's own use of words. Clearly, not all of the literary qualities noted here will be present in a single book, nor should gifted children be limited to reading books from Children's Choices or any other book list. They will profit from extensive reading of books identified by awards and by critics as well as superior works of literature not so designated.

By helping children to set criteria for judging books and by giving them opportunities to make their own decisions regarding book selection, we can begin to develop discriminating readers. Gifted children tend to be critical, not only of themselves but of objects and people in their environment. That natural sense of criticism can be the basis for developing a sense of quality in literature. The tendency toward self-criticism may be mitigated somewhat when children are able to relate to characters in books who also may be gifted or talented in some way or who seem to face the sorts of problems with which gifted children must deal. Similarly, children may become less critical of others who are not as intelligent or talented if they encounter sympathetically drawn characters in literature, characters who are developed in such a way that readers perceive their fears and shortcomings as real and not to be ridiculed. It seems natural that experiences with literature ought to take into account tendencies often associated with gifted children in order to turn them to a positive perspective whenever possible.

In addition to stimulating emotional and critical responses, a strong literature program will provide gifted children with opportunities to extend reading experiences to create their own oral and written expressions. It is here that the attention to structure and style can be realized as an important part of the literary experience for gifted and talented children. Furthermore, by giving children opportunities to create through dramatic as well as oral and written expression, we extend their recognition of the literary genres. Drawing attention to interrelationships between literature and the other art forms can help to establish early and lasting appreciation for literature.

The content and style of a book can have a powerful influence on a young reader. It is important to challenge children with the best books available so they have a sense of good literature. That suggests acquaintance with the variety of genres and pseudogenres represented in children's literature. In this chapter, we will deal with the pertinent types (excluding poetry, since a separate chapter focuses on poetry). The activities we plan to bring children together with books can also influence their responses. The selection of activities should be guided by an understanding of the literature to be read. What are the most important responses or ideas to be gained from a particular book or poem? How can we encourage children to interact with that piece of literature so the discussion or activity helps to promote understanding and response rather than overpowering the literary experience? The actual reading of the book or poem is the key experience. Beyond that, we can encourage other kinds of participation if we are sensitive to the effects of the experiences we design for that purpose.

Using Children's Choices Books with Gifted and Talented Children

An introduction to this section of the chapter is necessary. First, it is important to point out that the books included on the grids shown for younger and older children are simply representative. They are books from the 1976-1980 Children's Choices lists—books which might be used to generate responses to literature and which would appear to interest gifted children. However, new lists appear yearly, and it is expected that teachers and librarians will exercise their own judgment in adding and deleting books from this grid and from the accompanying suggested activities. These grids are *not* intended to represent a total literature program for gifted children; they are only suggestions for one part of a program. It is important to include experiences with other challenging books and poems (classics as well as contemporary works) and not limit children to those on Children's Choices lists.

Developing Responses of Younger Children

Laughter is a powerful emotional response to literature— a very personal response. Allen's *Mary Alice Operator Number 9* is a book likely to amuse most children and sophisticated enough in terms of illustrations to intrigue the gifted and talented. The most effective presentation is oral because much of the humor relies on vocal techniques, as cued by the use of italics, a variety of animal sounds such as "hisss," "woof," and "quack," and funny names such as Boss Chicken and Charlie Armadillo. A first oral reading should be followed by private viewing of the book so children can also appreciate the humor in Marshall's illustrations, for they add just the right touch to the incongruity of the situations that make up the story. A

Genres	Emotional/Personal Response	Interpretation	Literary Perception	Evaluative/Critical Response
Folk Literature	The Clown of God Strega Nona	North American Legends	Thorn Rose/Sleeping Beauty	Beauty and the Beast Nine at Carnival/Cinderella
Fantasy	The Bear's Bicycle George and Martha One Fine Day Bunnicula Owl at Home The Maggie B.	Bumps in the Night Dinner at Alberta's	Lambs for Dinner Portly McSwine	
Realistic Fiction	When the Wind Stops Maggie Marmelstein For President The New Girl at School	I Like the Library Max		The Great Brain Does It Again
Historical Fiction		Merry Ever After All the Children Were Sent Away		
Biography		What's the Big Idea, Ben Franklin?		
Information Books	Dollhouse Magic Roman Numerals The Popcorn Book			Small Worlds Close Up
Structure Books	Mr. and Mrs. Pig's Evening Out	Paddy Pork's Holiday	Deep in the Forest Hiccup	
Poetry	Make a Circle Keep Us In	Stopping by Woods On A Snowy Evening	Near the Window Tree	

Monson

leading question, asking children what was the silliest thing about the story, and a second, asking what they liked best about Mary Alice herself, should elicit plenty of discussion. The logical follow up would be to encourage children to interpret the story orally. In order to do that successfully, they will have to study each character, deciding how Jake Dog, Connie Hyena, and the rest might have felt and then translating their feelings into the sounds they made. Children who have worked out effective oral interpretations might enjoy reading the story to younger children or to their parents.

Role playing can also help to involve children emotionally with a story. Delton's *The New Girl at School* develops a situation which most children fear and many experience. There are many possibilities for enhancing involvement with Marcia in the story. After it has been read to the children (or read independently), ask them to describe how Marcia might feel if she were new to their school, or set up a situation in which one child plays the role of Marcia and another takes the part of an "old student" in the class. Encourage the children to generate a conversation in which a new child asks questions about the school and the teacher, seeking answers that will help make adjustment easier. Playing and observing both roles can open children's eyes to the responsibilities they have toward a child who is new to a school.

Maggie Marmelstein for President, by Sharmat, offers good material for more sophisticated role playing and interpretation. Maggie appears bossy and overbearing, yet she emerges as an extremely able little girl. Gifted and talented children who are involved in struggles for leadership may enjoy playing Maggie's role as campaign manager. There are a number of passages in the story that are well suited to oral interpretation or Readers Theatre because of the well-written dialogue. You might select one passage and let children choose the character parts they want to play (not forgetting to add a narrator for the crucial narrative sections). The success of the reading will depend on prior study of the characters, thinking about the goals and circumstances that motivate them to think, behave, and speak as they do.

Another kind of emotional response is that triggered by curiosity. Informational books such as de Paola's *The Popcorn Book*, Adler's *Roman Numerals*, and Roche's *Dollhouse Magic* can engage the curiosity of gifted and talented children. *The Popcorn Book* may lead to an independent search for information about other phenomena that whet the reader's curiosity. *Roman Numerals* may encourage children to try to devise other numbering systems or perhaps to investigate the way a computer works. *Dollhouse Magic* will give some children incentive to try to produce some of the items described. These extensions are natural and help to give nonfiction a place in their lives.

The experiences described next depend on interpretation of character roles and story situations as means of extending the emotional response generated by a book. *Strega Nona* is a folktale retold by de Paola. The story builds to quite an intensity, and it involves two key characters, Strega Nona and Big Anthony. Big Anthony has not quite mastered Strega Nona's magic and therefore is unable to stop her magic pot, once he has made it produce pasta. Children enjoy interpreting Big Anthony's thoughts and motives and recognizing how he changes in mood from the beginning to the end of the book. Each child can retell the story, learning the art of storytelling through the experience. At the same time, the storyteller develops a sense of the way excitement builds as the story goes along and gains a sort of satisfaction with the resolution of the problem. Children who enjoy telling *Strega Nona* may want to try their hand at other folktales found among the Children's Choices books.

Literary understanding may also grow through active involvement with books. Such understanding includes recognition of form and structure, characterization, description, and the quality of a writer's or illustrator's style. It is not necessary for younger children (even those who are identified as gifted and talented) to spend a great deal of time with literary analysis. However, some qualities of literature will be relatively easy and interesting for them to grasp. An example is the stylistic effect of play on words. *Portly McSwine* by Marshall and *Bunnicula* by the Howes will amuse and may also motivate children to try creating other funny titles based on word play. An especially intriguing title may even inspire a whole story.

A sense of structure was mentioned earlier as one of the characteristics frequently noted in gifted children. Perhaps that is why they often delight in recognizing folktales that share underlying themes and structures. There are a number of such tales among the Children's Choices books, tales which may be paired with derivatives from other countries or with retellings to give children opportunities to compare the versions and see how they are alike as well as different. For that purpose, Lloyd's *Nine at Carnival*, a Jamaican tale, can be paired with Galdone's *Cinderella*. Children will enjoy contrasting the settings as well as the plots of the stories. Evaluation comes in when they try to decide which version they like better and whether the Jamaican version is essentially the same story as *Cinderella*, even though there are rather marked differences. LeCain's *Thorn Rose* and Hyman's *The Sleeping Beauty*, though more alike in setting, will also provoke thoughtful comparison and give opportunity to evaluate the two versions for the most satisfying telling and support their decisions. Discussing several folktale versions can lead to examination of fantasy with a strong folktale theme. An example of this is Maestro's *Lambs for Dinner*. The story itself is charming. Enjoyment may be increased for some children by a reading of the old tale, "The Wolf and the Seven Little Kids," which can be found in most folktale anthologies. Children will quickly recognize that the plots and characters are similar. As a result, they may want to try to create their own contemporary fantasy stories modeled after familiar folktales.

Recognition of basic plot structure can develop from comparison and discussion of folktales. It can also develop through experiences with wordless picture books. Just as *Lambs for Dinner* is related to a folktale, so is Turkle's *Deep in the Forest*, a wordless book from the Children's Choices list. Children may tell or even write a story to go along with Turkle's fine illustrations. As they interpret the pictures, they will quickly realize that the story is an inversion of Goldilocks, in which a little lost bear wanders into a human home. Children enjoy the incongruity arising from this "translation" of the old story. Telling or writing the story gives excellent experience in picture interpretation and in telling a story from start to finish.

Two other Children's Choices books without words also provide good material for prewriting oral expression or for early writing experience. Mayer's *Hiccup* and Goodall's *Paddy*

Pork's Holiday have captivating illustrations that show complete enough stories to motivate good storytelling and writing. The details in the pictures are important, so children should be reminded to let their words tell as much about setting and characters as they can manage. Some children will enjoy inserting dialogue into their stories in order to show more vividly what the characters are like and then to share the story with various audiences.

Developing Responses of Older Gifted Children

With older children, as with younger ones, the personal/emotional response to a book is most important. The emotional response may come naturally just from reading a book. In some cases, it can be strengthened when children have special experiences such as discussing a book, role playing the part of a character, presenting part of it in a Readers Theatre setting, or using the book as inspiration for their own writing.

Words by Heart by Sebestyen is an emotionally charged book, and it brings strong response from readers. Episode by episode, the book encourages the reader to try to perceive the scene from the point of view of one of the story characters. The opening scene is a good example, as the Bible memory contest goes on and on between Lena and Winslow Starnes. What thoughts are in Winslow's mind as the contest draws to a close? In Lena's mind? In Jaybird Kelsey's? Such discussion based on point of view is most effective after children have read the entire story so they have characters and problems in perspective. Some reactions to this story may be too personal for discussion so it is best to simply accept comments children offer but not to probe into their personal reactions.

The matter of curiosity as an emotional response was mentioned earlier. Older gifted children exhibit curiosity about a tremendous range of topics, and they gain emotional satisfaction from learning more about those topics. *The Code and Cipher Book* by Sarnoff and Ruffins is one that will provoke curiosity and stimulate interest in trying out codes as well as producing and using new ones. Children who are interested may also want to learn the braille alphabet and/or become acquainted with signing used by deaf people. *Handtalk* (not a Children's Choice book but listed in the bibliography) is a good source for the latter.

Genres	Emotional/Personal Response	Interpretation	Literary Perception	Evaluative/ Critical Response
Folk Literature		The Stonecutter The Sorcerer's Apprentice	Why Mosquitoes Buzz in People's Ears	Beauty and the Beast
Fantasy	Mice on My Mind Lizard Music		A Swiftly Tilting Planet Tuck Everlasting	
Realistic Fiction	Sideways Stories from Wayside School The Pistachio Prescription Absolute Zero Can You Sue Your Parents for Malpractice?	Frozen Fire Your Old Pal, Al Good-Bye Chicken Little Words by Heart	Father's Arcane Daughter	Alan Mendelsohn, The Boy from Mars Anastasia Krupnick
Historical Fiction	Journey Home The Borrowed House	The Man With the Silver Eyes	Going Back	Dragonwings
Biography	Jacques Cousteau How I Came to Be a Writer			
Information Books	The Code and Cipher Book Model Buildings and How to Make Them	How to Turn Lemons into Money Pyramid		Underground Habitats
Poetry/ Drama	Nightmares: Poems to Trouble Your Sleep The Desert Is Theirs	Is There an Actor in the House?		

Danziger's *The Pistachio Prescription* evokes considerable personal response from readers. Some children identify with Cassie; others are able to sympathize with her. The book is a natural for questions such as, "How are you, your family, and your friends like the people in this story? Can you learn anything about yourself by knowing Cassie?" Many episodes provide good discussion material. The book is not all serious, though, and children respond to the humorous dialogue as well. Some passages with a good deal of dialogue will adapt well to oral interpretation in the form of Readers Theatre.

Cresswell's *Absolute Zero* and Pinkwater's *Lizard Music* contain a considerable amount of humor. Children will enjoy sharing favorite passages by reading them aloud to other students. Preparing for the oral reading gives good opportunity to interpret humorous sections, deciding why they are funny and what techniques the author used to produce the humor. Further, children have the opportunity to experiment with vocal interpretation in order to decide how to convey humor most effectively when they read aloud. Although the focus here is on the emotional reaction to humor, the steps leading to children's oral reading will also involve interpretation and awareness of literary quality.

The humor in *Sideways Stories from Wayside School* by Sacher will appeal to some children in the older group and to others who are younger. It is based on a sense of incongruity with a liberal dose of slapstick. Children who enjoy this humor will be interested in trying to explain *why* the stories are funny. They may want to consider these kinds of literary humor: play on words, laughter at a character, surprising or impossible situations, and ridiculous or incongruous situations. They can reread each story in this collection and try to decide what major type of humor is represented. They may also want to try to determine which of the stories is the funniest. Because most children have had experiences in school not unlike some described in this book, they may want to write their own humorous stories to put into a collection.

The appeal of emotional involvement as well as character interpretation carries over to script reading. Bradley's *Is There an Actor in the House?* provides opportunity for Readers Theatre script reading (oral interpretation without the use of staging and actions) or for scripts memorized and used for dramatic productions complete with scenery. Children will want to work as a group to decide which of the plays to produce. They will probably need some guidance in character interpretation as they examine motives and feelings of the characters they are to play, using whatever information the script provides.

Historical fiction, such as Yep's *Dragonwings*, provides for a wide range of responses. Certainly, children identify emotionally with Moon Shadow and, to some extent, with his father, Windrider. They can try to interpret the social milieu of the time by comparing Moon Shadow's life with their own lives. They can begin to understand universals of the human condition by comparing Moon Shadow's hopes and fears with their own and his father's great drive to achieve his goal with the behavior of adults they know. Historical fiction suggests a special incentive for children to read critically. Historical accuracy is of utmost importance to the quality of the story. Children should be encouraged to seek nonfiction accounts of the San Francisco of Moon Shadow's day so they can see how carefully Laurence Yep carried out research for the background of his story.

The Ghost Belonged to Me by Peck is another book with a historical setting that will capture children's interest in the period. Though not truly historical fiction, the book is set in the early 1900s. Setting, characters, and language are all reminiscent of that period in history. Students may be challenged to try to determine which aspects of the story are historically realistic and which are not. (The ghost should give them a clue!)

L'Engle's *A Swiftly Tilting Planet* brings readers back to the characters they knew in *A Wrinkle in Time*. Meeting Meg and Calvin grown up gives the story an interesting perspective and leads to many questions about the relationship between the two stories. Did Meg and Calvin grow up to be the kinds of people we would have expected from our knowledge of them as children? What problems did they face then? What are their concerns now? Thinking over both books, what underlying theme or themes is the author developing? Is the last book more pessimistic than the first? Children will have their own comments and questions, too, and may conclude the discussion by making a judgment as to which of the books they like better.

Another book of fantasy, Babbitt's *Tuck Everlasting*, deserves special attention from gifted and talented children because of the author's style and superb description of setting and mood. A sensitive oral reading of the first few pages of chapter one, either by the teacher or by a student, can serve as the basis for a discussion about the mood that is set and the way in which descriptive words and sentence length contribute to that mood. Let children make note of the descriptions they find most interesting throughout the book and read their favorite sections to classmates.

Folktales, too, can help to make children aware of literary qualities. Aardema's *Why Mosquitoes Buzz in People's Ears* has a stylistic quality that is enhanced when it is read aloud and is made even more dramatic when the oral reading is accompanied by pantomime of the animals so that it becomes story theater.[2] Children will also enjoy comparing the tale with porquoi tales from other parts of the world.

The Sorcerer's Apprentice is another folktale that can inspire response to the structure of a tale. An oral reading will reveal the great increase in pace as the story builds toward a climax. When the frightened apprentice chops the broom in half, the action doubles and continues at that pace until the sorcerer returns home and puts things right. It is interesting to use this story to show children how old tales have inspired composers to write music. If a recording of *The Sorcerer's Apprentice* is available, children will enjoy identifying the themes that represent various elements in the story, especially the wild movements of the broom(s). Those who are particularly interested in the relationship of music to literature will also enjoy hearing recordings of ballet music set to the stories of *The Sleeping Beauty, The Nutcracker*, and *Scheherazade*.

Nonfiction can serve as material for many kinds of responses, with curiosity often a dominant one. Gifted children need to learn to evaluate nonfiction so they can appreciate accuracy and clarity of presentation. *Underground* is a good book for encouraging such evaluation. These children should begin to be aware of the qualifications authors bring to nonfiction. Macaulay's credentials are impressive and can be appreciated by children. In order to decide whether he has conveyed his information clearly in this book, children might want to seek other sources for comparison or try to explain to one another some of the objects underground and their functions. As follow-up they will undoubtedly want to read Macaulay's other books and, perhaps, use the information to try to create models of the structures he presents.

Armstrong's *How to Turn Lemons into Money* is a humorous rather than a serious treatment of economics. Nevertheless, there is much information within the compact volume. A good means of evaluating clarity and completeness of the information would be for children to try to apply the terms used to describe business in a lemonade stand to another kind of business, writing and illustrating their descriptions of economics in the new situation.

Extending Reading from Children's Choices Books to Other Books

Gifted and talented children will be interested to learn that each year a number of lists of recommended books are published. They already may be aware of the Newbery and Caldecott Award Books and Honor Books. Another annual list to bring to their attention is the American Library Association's list of Notable Books. Children who are provided with the Children's Choices lists for each year and with the ALA Notable Books and Newbery/Caldecott books will find it interesting to see which Children's Choices books appear on one or both of the other lists. When they have identified some, they might be encouraged to read as many of the books as possible, keeping in mind these questions: Why would children choose the book? What is there about it that appeals to me, as a child? Why would adults choose the book for a special list or award? Does it have especially good characterization? Are the descriptions vivid? Is the plot interesting? Is it clear that all parts of the book, including characters and episodes, fit into the overall plot structure and work together for the total effect? Does the author's style suit the mood of the story? Does the book read well aloud? Are the illustrations unusually attractive, interesting, and right for the story? Is it clear that the author is trying to convey a definite idea or message through the book?

Some books which appear on both the Children's Choices and the ALA Notable Books lists are included here.

The Bear's Bicycle by Emilie Warren McLeod
Deep in the Forest by Brinton Turkle
Dinner at Alberta's by Russell Hoban
Frog and Toad All Year by Arnold Lobel
The Maggie B. by Irene Haas
Max by Rachel Isadora
Merry Ever After by Joe Lasker
Owl at Home by Arnold Lobel
Strega Nona: An Old Tale retold by Tomie de Paola

INTERMEDIATE
The Desert is Theirs by Byrd Baylor
Dragonwings by Laurence Yep
The Ghost Belonged to Me by Richard Peck
Pyramid by David Macaulay
Why Mosquitoes Buzz in People's Ears by Verna Aardema

Another means of extending reading from Children's Choices books to others involves a focus on authors. When children find a Children's Choices book that is particularly enjoyable, encourage them to read all other available books by that author and decide which they like best and why. Children may also want to see whether an author or illustrator has a theme that is evident in more than one book (see Madeline L'Engle or Susan Cooper) or a style that is identifiable (see James Marshall, William Steig, or David Macaulay). Many of the authors and illustrators whose books appear on Children's Choices lists have published other books, offering almost limitless possibility as an ongoing project.

The suggestions in this chapter for involving gifted and talented children with Children's Choices books are certainly not all-inclusive, nor are the books discussed here the only ones that will provide challenge to these children. Teachers who are readers themselves will continue to discover books to add to the curriculum. In the end, the goal is to introduce all children to a variety of books and to encourage their responses so that literature takes a firm and lasting place in their lives, becoming a key to new knowledge and a source of inspiration and comfort through good and bad times.

Footnotes

[1] The kinds of responses described in this chapter are based on those identified by Alan C. Purves and Victoria Rippere in *Elements of writing about a literary work: A study of response to literature.* Urbana, Illinois: NCTE, 1968.

[2] For a discussion of this technique, see *Children and books, sixth edition.* Glenview, Illinois: Scott, Foresman, 1981.

Books for Younger Children

Adler, David. *Roman Numerals.* Illustrated by Byron Barton. New York: Thomas Y. Crowell, 1977.

Adoff, Arnold. *Make a Circle Keep Us In: Poems for a Good Day.* Illustrated by Ronald Himler. New York: Delacorte, 1975.

Allard, Harry. *Bumps in the Night.* New York: Doubleday, 1979.

Allen, Jeffrey. *Mary Alice Operator Number 9.* Illustrated by James Marshall. Boston: Little, Brown, 1975.

de Paola, Tomie. *Strega Nona.* Englewood Cliffs, New Jersey: Prentice-Hall, 1975.

de Paola, Tomie. *The Clown of God.* New York: Harcourt Brace Jovanovich, 1978.

de Paola, Tomie. *The Popcorn Book.* New York: Holiday House, 1978.

Delton, Judy. *The New Girl at School.* New York: E.P. Dutton, 1979.

Fritz, Jean. *Where Was Patrick Henry on the 29th of May?* Illustrated by Margot Tomes. New York: Coward, McCann & Geoghegan, 1975.

Fritz, Jean. *What's the Big Idea, Ben Franklin?* Illustrated by Margot Tomes. New York: Coward, McCann & Geoghegan, 1977.

Fitzgerald, John D. *The Great Brain Does It Again.* Illustrated by Mercer Mayer. New York: Dial Press, 1975.

Frost, Robert. *Stopping by Woods on a Snowy Evening.* Illustrated by Susan Jeffers. New York: E.P. Dutton, 1978.

Gag, Wanda. *The Sorcerer's Apprentice.* New York: Coward, McCann & Geoghegan, 1979.

Galdone, Paul (retold by). *Cinderella.* New York: McGraw-Hill, 1978.

Garrigue, Sheila. *All the Children Were Sent Away.* Scarsdale, New York: Bradbury, 1977.

*Goffstein, M.B. *Fish for Supper.* New York: Dial Press, 1976.

Goodall, John S. *Paddy Pork's Holiday.* New York: Atheneum/McElderry, 1976.

Grillone, Lisa, & Gennaro, Joseph. *Small Worlds Close Up.* New York: Crown, 1978.

Haas, Irene. *The Maggie B.* New York: Atheneum/McElderry, 1975.

Haviland, Virginia (selected by). *North American Legends.* Illustrated by Ann Strugnell. New York: Philomel Books, 1979.

Hoban, Russell. *Dinner at Alberta's.* Illustrated by James Marshall. New York: Thomas Y. Crowell, 1975.

Howe, Deborah & Howe, James. *Bunnicula.* Illustrated by Alan Daniel. New York: Atheneum, 1979.

Hyman, Trina Shart (retold by). *The Sleeping Beauty.* Boston: Little, Brown, 1977.

Isadora, Rachel. *Max.* New York: Macmillan, 1976.

Kuskin, Karla. *Near the Window Tree: Poems and Notes.* New York: Harper & Row, 1975.

---

* Not on the Children's Choices list but an ALA Notable Book.

Lasker, Joe. *Merry Ever After*. New York: Viking, 1976.

LeCain, E. (illustrator). *Thorn Rose or the Sleeping Beauty*. Scarsdale, New York: Bradbury, 1977.

Lloyd, Errol. *Nine at Carnival*. New York: Thomas Y. Crowell, 1979.

Lobel, Arnold. *Owl at Home*. New York: Harper & Row, 1975.

Lobel, Arnold. *Frog and Toad All Year*. New York: Harper & Row, 1976.

Maestro, Betsy. *Lambs for Dinner*. New York: Crown, 1978.

Marshall, James. *George and Martha One Fine Day*. Boston: Houghton Mifflin, 1978.

Marshall, James. *Portly McSwine*. Boston: Houghton Mifflin, 1979.

Mayer, Marianna (retold by). *Beauty and the Beast*. Illustrated by Mercer Mayer. New York: Scholastic, 1978.

Mayer, Mercer. *Hiccup*. New York: Dial, 1976.

McLeod, Emilie Warren. *The Bear's Bicycle*. Boston: Little, Brown, 1975.

Rayner, Mary. *Mr. and Mrs. Pig's Evening Out*. New York: Atheneum, 1976.

Roche, P.K. *Dollhouse Magic: How to Make and Find Simple Dollhouse Furniture*. Photos by John Knott. Illustrated by Richard Cuffari. New York: Dial, 1977.

Rockwell, Anne. *I Like the Library*. New York: E.P. Dutton, 1977.

Sharmat, Marjorie. *Maggie Marmelstein for President*. Illustrated by Ben Schechter. New York: Harper & Row, 1975.

*Steig, William. *Abel's Island*. New York: Farrar, Straus & Giroux, 1976.

*Steig, William. *The Amazing Bone*. New York: Farrar, Straus & Giroux, 1976.

*Tripp, Wallace. *Granfa' Grig Had a Pig and Other Rhymes without Reason from Mother Goose*. Boston: Little, Brown, 1976.

Turkle, Brinton. *Deep in the Forest*. New York: E.P. Dutton, 1976.

Zolotow, Charlotte. *When the Wind Stops*. Illustrated by Howard Knotts. New York: Harper & Row, 1975.

Books for Older Children

Aardema, Verna. *Why Mosquitoes Buzz in People's Ears*. Illustrated by Leo and Diane Dillon. New York: Dial, 1975.

Armstrong, Louise. *How to Turn Lemons into Money*. Illustrated by Bill Basso. New York: Harcourt Brace Jovanovich, 1976.

Babbitt, Natalie. *Tuck Everlasting*. New York: Farrar, Straus & Giroux, 1978.

Baylor, Byrd. *The Desert Is Theirs*. Illustrated by Peter Parnell. New York: Scribner's, 1975.

Baylor, Byrd. *Hawk, I'm Your Brother*. New York: Scribner's, 1976.

Bradley, Virginia. *Is There an Actor in the House?* New York: Dodd, Mead, 1975.

Byars, Betsy. *Good-Bye, Chicken Little*. New York: Scholastic Book Services, 1979.

Charlip, Remy, Ancona, Mary Beth, & Ancona, George. *Handtalk*. New York: Parent's Magazine Press, 1974.

Cleaver, Vera, & Cleaver, Bill. *Trial Valley*. New York: Lippincott, 1977.

*Cooper, Susan. *The Grey King*. New York: Atheneum, 1976.

Cresswell, Helen. *Absolute Zero*. New York: Macmillan, 1978.

Danziger, Paula. *The Pistachio Prescription*. New York: Delacorte, 1978.

Danziger, Paula. *Can You Sue Your Parents for Malpractice?* New York: Delacorte, 1979.

---

* Not on the Children's Choices list but an ALA Notable Book.

*Flanagan, Geraldine Lux, & Morris, Sean. *Window into a Nest*. Boston: Houghton Mifflin, 1975.
Green, Constance C. *Your Old Pal, Al*. New York: Viking, 1979.
Hess, Hila. *Small Habitats*. New York: Scribner's, 1976.
Houston, James. *Frozen Fire*. New York: Atheneum, 1977.
Iverson, Genie. *Jacques Cousteau*. Illustrated by Hal Ashmead. New York: Putnam's, 1976.
Konigsburg, E.L. *Father's Arcane Daughter*. New York: Atheneum, 1976.
L'Engle, Madeleine. *A Swiftly Tilting Planet*. New York: Farrar, Straus & Giroux, 1978.
Lively, Penelope. *Going Back*. New York: E.P. Dutton, 1975.
Lowry, Lois. *Anastasia Krupnick*. Boston: Houghton Mifflin, 1979.
Macaulay, David. *Pyramid*. Boston: Houghton Mifflin, 1975.
Macaulay, David. *Underground*. Boston: Houghton Mifflin, 1976.
*Mathis, Sharon Bell. *The Hundred Penny Box*. New York: Viking, 1975.
Mayer, Marianna (retold by). *Beauty and the Beast*. Illustrated by Mercer Mayer. New York: Four Winds Press, 1978.
McDermott, Gerald. *The Stonecutter*. New York: Viking, 1975.
Naylor, Phyllis. *How I Came to Be a Writer*. New York: Atheneum, 1978.
*O'Dell, Scott. *Zia*. Boston: Houghton Mifflin, 1976.
Pinkwater, D. Manus. *Lizard Music*. New York: Dodd, Mead, 1976.
Pinkwater, D. Manus. *Alan Mendelsohn, The Boy from Mars*. New York: E.P. Dutton, 1979.
Sacher, Louis. *Sideways Stories from Wayside School*. Illustrated by Dennis Hockerman. New York: Follett, 1978.
Sarnoff, Jane, & Ruffins, Reynold. *The Code and Cipher Book*. New York: Scribner's, 1975.
Sebestyen, Ouida. *Words by Heart*. New York: Bantam Books, 1979.
Steele, William. *The Man with the Silver Eyes*. New York: Harcourt Brace Jovanovich, 1976.
Uchida, Yoshiko. *Journey Home*. New York: Atheneum/McElderry, 1978.
Von Stockum, Hilda. *The Borrowed House*. New York: Farrar, Straus & Giroux, 1975.
Waber, Bernard. *Mice on My Mind*. Boston: Houghton Mifflin, 1977.
Yep, Laurence. *Dragonwings*. New York: Harper & Row, 1975.

---

* Not on the Children's Choices list but an ALA Notable Book.

Choosing Poetry

Sam Leaton Sebesta
University of Washington

The annual Children's Choices lists make good reading. They offer clues to children's interests and tastes in literature and they include sample responses and ideas for activities. The information the lists provide about children's choices in poetry is of special interest to me.

These poetry preferences are not at all what studies would lead us to expect. Typically, studies have consistently revealed children's preferences for humor, action, story line, and topics related closely to everyday experiences (Fisher & Natarella, 1979; Nelson, 1966; Terry, 1974). Further, these studies indicated children's affinity for nonsense: intermediate graders especially liked the limerick form. Almost without exception, research has substantiated children's preferences for poetry that rhymes and has regular meter. In contrast, poetry that children disliked was serious, lyric rather than narrative, sometimes abstract, often with highly figurative language and extended imagery. Neither did children favor poems without rhyme and meter; they eschewed blank verse and free verse. Two of the studies (Terry, 1974; Tom, 1969) noted that children liked recently written poems, rather than those written for past generations.

But poetry preferences disclosed in the Children's Choices lists do not fit these characteristic profiles. They include many traditional poems. For example, intermediate graders liked the 11 episodes of Martin's *Old Mother Hubbard and Her Dog*, first published in 1805, and a newly cartooned edition of Riley's "Little Orphant Annie," first published a century ago.* They liked some serious traditional poems, as evident in Adoff's collection, *My Black Me: A Beginning Book of Black Poetry*. Surprisingly, the students approved Frost's *Stopping by Woods on a Snowy Evening*. Previous studies have placed Frost and Carl Sandburg on lists of disliked poets.

---

* Poetry titles referred to in this chapter are listed with bibliographic information at the end of the chapter.

Serious poetry, blank and free verse, and extended imagery—all qualities that children disapproved in other preference studies—are present on the lists of Children's Choices. They liked, for example, the personified desert in Byrd Baylor's *The Desert is Theirs*:

> The desert gives
> what it can
> to each of its children.

From Byrd Baylor. *The Desert Is Theirs*. Illustrated by Peter Parnall. New York: Scribner's, 1975. Text copyright © 1975 Byrd Baylor; illustrations copyright © 1975 Peter Parnall.

Karla Kuskin and Myra Cohn Livingston, both experimenters in blank and free verse, are on the favored list. Arnold Adoff's tone poem *Tornado!* is in free verse form and serious, but children chose it. The exquisite *More Small Poems* by Valerie Worth won admiration.

SAFETY PIN

> Closed, it sleeps
> On its side
> Quietly,
> The silver
> Image
> Of some
> Small fish;
>
> Opened, it snaps
> Its tail out
> Like a thin
> Shrimp, and looks
> At the sharp
> Point with a
> Surprised eye.

Reprinted by permission of Farrar, Straus and Giroux, Inc. "Safety Pin" from *More Small Poems* by Valerie Worth. Pictures by Natalie Babbitt. Text copyright © 1976 by Valerie Worth.

Furthermore, children who comprised the Children's Choices sample demonstrated greater affection for poetry than has been apparent in the recent past. Moray (1978) cites a study in which poetry ranked eighth among nine types of reading available to children. (Only social studies reading material ranked lower in their esteem.) A Canadian survey by Ashley (1972) places poetry twelfth among thirteen categories for children in grades four through seven. Yet, the ratio of poetry choices to the number of poetry books available in the Children's Choices project indicates stronger approval. Only one type of poetry book seems to be excluded from those children approved for Children's Choices: the lengthy "heavy" anthology composed of a large selection of poems unified by topic of theme.

No doubt there are many reasons for the discrepancy between Children's Choices results and other studies' results. I will suggest only three of them.

1. Most other studies present poetry to children in brief, abrupt fashion. Often a group of poems is read aloud once or twice, and students are asked to indicate which of the poems they love, which ones they are indifferent to, and which ones they hate. The resulting data tell us about *instant* preferences. Perhaps we should not be surprised that these data collection techniques tend to record forced options rather than reflect taste and real interests. We may be doing children a disservice when we assume that quick preferences are an accurate assessment of all they like in poetry.

By contrast, poetry books circulated as part of the Children's Choices selection process are available over a period of time—two to six weeks in most classrooms. They can be thumbed through and gone back to. There is time for children to make discoveries, think them over, and let them grow or wane in their esteem.

2. Most other studies present poetry to children orally and, indeed, most texts and articles recommend that poetry be presented in this way. Yet the printed poem, with its unique arrangement on the page, and accompanying illustrations, may have a visual impact that, in itself, has power to arouse the reader. Poetry books selected by readers often enough to be included in the Children's Choices lists frequently contain one poem or one stanza per page, generously spaced and tastefully illustrated. In fact, visual appeal may account for some of the differences in results between this survey and other studies.

3. Most other studies tend not to reflect the balance in poetry teaching that may have resulted from the merging of structure study and a response-to-literature emphasis. It is fair

to suggest that our methods of presenting poetry in the classroom have changed and improved over the past few years. The 1960s brought numerous projects and texts that asked young readers to analyze poetry, sometimes in prescriptive ways: rhyme schemes, paraphrase, imagery analysis, explicit statements about the poet's tone or mood. With the 1970s came a shift toward "literary experience," inviting readers' open responses rather than analysis. Perhaps what we are seeing in the Children's Choices poetry preferences is, in part, the welcome result of both efforts: attention to how a poem works and encouragement to respond.

Each of these three reasons has implications for teaching. Each helps to focus the suggestions which make up the rest of this chapter.

Finding Poetry

In classrooms where children are excited about poetry, teachers are encouraging children and young people to explore collections of poetry. They display poetry books randomly about the classroom or on the reading table. They give time for browsing, for scanning to find a collection that appeals, and for skimming to locate a poem that has an interest-catching topic or line.

They find time to talk about how to explore a selection—how to "bite right in" and read with full attention, reading and rereading, regressing to pick up lines and phrases that invite reading aloud to test the sound, or pausing to "see" an image.

The successful teachers point out that all reading rates as well as all levels of attention apply to reading poetry. Linear readers, accustomed to following from start to finish the accumulating trail of narrative in a novel, get help to develop the flexibility needed for reading poetry. The teacher demonstrates this flexibility: the browsing, the skimming, the ultimate care devoted to a specific selection. One way in which this flexibility is demonstrated is through display of a selection on a chalkboard, tagboard chart, or overhead projector. Students then find lines or phrases that the poet clearly intends to be read aloud, such as Karla Kuskin's simple but indelible line about birds who "ease into a passing breeze" (p. 37). The teacher shows how a silent reader reading independently has the leisure to pause to test sound or see an image. Like good drivers, poetry readers are able to say to themselves: *Slow down—a scenic view is here!* Try, for example, to decide where good poetry readers would pause to reflect on sound or image as they read this stanza from Kuskin:

> The flow of a cat walking
> Over the lawn
> To place herself like a soft stone
> In the middle of the paper
> I am working on.
>
> From *Near the Window Tree* by Karla Kuskin. Copyright © 1975 by Karla Kuskin. Reprinted by permission of Harper & row, Publishers, Inc.

In the past, close reading of poetry got a bad name. Too often it turned into an inquisition. Readers were directed to spot a simile, mine a metaphor, or dissect a rhyme scheme. Now the intent is different. It is to encourage close reading so that independent readers can give good poetry the time, attention, and reflection needed for literary experience.

Once readers are comfortable with flexibility,* teachers who are poetry sharers bring in the dinosaur-sized anthologies that only educators have dared to touch. Free of the constraint of having to read linearly from page 1 to page 600, children are now able to browse through the heavy volumes to pursue their quest for poetry.

Traditional poetry in these anthologies may win its place in the children's affections, too: works of Dorothy Aldis, Elizabeth Coatsworth, A.A. Milne, Walter de la Mare, Carl Sandburg, and James Reeves, to name a few.

When children are encouraged to share their discoveries and to discuss them, satisfaction with poetry spreads. A good technique is to divide a class into pairs rather than to try to hold a discussion in which one speaks to the entire group. In this way, everyone has intimate opportunity to participate in sharing poetry.

---

* A not-to-be-ignored side effect is flexibility in reading prose, especially descriptive prose with its own nuances and rhythms. In fact, the work of many good authors of fiction (e.g., Phillippa Pearce, Paula Fox, L.M. Boston) possesses the characteristics of blank verse.

Interpreting Poetry

A half century ago textbooks on how to interpret poetry were quite common (Gullon, 1931). The questions posed concerned manner of delivery: "Is your soft palate relaxed enough for vowels? Is hands-behind-the-back the best posture for recitation?" Elocution techniques were stressed, including correct pronunciation, enunciation, and articulation. Sometimes the authors of these texts wrote poetry to give students practice with the techniques, and sometimes poetry was selected from other sources for its appropriateness as an elocution exercise.

When considered today, such attention to manner of delivery rather than the message itself seems to have been misdirected. Nowadays the training of actors and amateurs alike begins with meaning, not with sound. It begins with close reading, with inner rather than outer interpretation. Only after the meaning has been apprehended does the poetry reader attempt to communicate the poem orally.

There are pitfalls in both approaches. Elocution could lead to empty performance—sound without substance. Modern meaning-based delivery can require so much analysis of a poem's tone and message that enjoyment and spontaneity are lost. But to neglect interpretation entirely, to treat poetry reading as just another opportunity for oral reading practice, is to miss the excitement of genuine literary experience. Here, then, are some suggestions that have been successful for enlivening poems through oral interpretation.

1. Whatever the grade level, it is best to begin with humorous verse and probably with unison choric speaking. Why? Humor has instant appeal. It immediately invites sharing. Its demands upon interpretation are usually clear and broad. Choric speaking, although considered the most difficult oracy art by the elocutionists, gives group solidarity that supports individual risk-taking later. It is a way of sharing and enjoying, and a natural outgrowth of the rhymes and jingles of the nursery.

Children's Choices poems appropriate for such choric speaking in its early stages include Zuromskis' *The Farmer in the Dell* and Lobel's *Gregory Griggs and Other Nursery Rhyme People* at the primary level; Lee's *Alligator Pie* and

Prelutsky's *The Mean Old Mean Hyena* at the intermediate level; and the more subtle word-play humor of Orgel's *Merry Merry FIBruary* and Gardner's *The Child's Bestiary* are appropriate at intermediate and upper levels. Shorter items can be done as "echo poems": a leader models the poem by reading it aloud or reciting it from memory and the group repeats it, adding force and excitement to enliven the rendition. Although no one is assigned to memorize a poem, it is not unusual to find that echo-type choric speaking results in memorization without conscious effort.

Variations and additions to unison choric speaking usually suggest themselves. Zuromskis' *The Farmer in the Dell* invites simultaneous "acting out" as the chorus chants the rhyme, and oral interpretation catches the liveliness of such physical response. The cast of characters from Prelutsky's *The Mean Old Mean Hyena* (see box) is quoted directly, so that sub-groups or individuals may logically take those direct quote lines.

The Mean Old Mean Hyena by Jack Prelutsky. Illustrated by Arnold Lobel. Greenwillow, 1978.

Parts

Narrators—3 to divide the narration among them
Hyena   Ostrich
Zebra   Lion
Elephant
Chorus—to do the refrain

What to Do

1. Figure out, ahead of time, variations in pace: which verses must be fast and tricky, and which need to be slow so that the listeners are given time to wonder what will happen next.
2. Emphasize repeated consonant sounds (alliteration): *lazy, lanky, lean, sneaky, slinky,* etc.
3. Emphasize verbs: *chuckled, chortled*; "He *jeered* and *frolicked, cheered* and *roared*."

After this, it is only a step to other divisions. For instance, the punch line in this verse from Gardner's *The*

Child's Bestiary gets a special effect if an individual delivers it after the group's solemn delivery of the lines that precede it:

> Always be kind to animals,
> Morning, noon, and night;
> For animals have feelings too,
> And furthermore, they bite.

From *A Child's Bestiary* by John Gardner, illustrated by Lucy, Joel, Joan, and John Gardner. Copyright 1977 by Alfred A Knopf, Inc.

Choric speaking used in this nonthreatening way is a good prelude to individual oral interpretation. Single-speaker poems with a unified light tone may follow. The hurried, worried couplet ending with surprise in the title poem in Bodecker's *Hurry, Hurry, Mary Dear!* are just right for one or more fledgling readers who will benefit from the experience of enlivening a poem before a small audience. And this poem, like many others, can be combined with story theatre; i.e., a couple of actors mime the action as the speaker reads. Primary-level children can make page-by-page individual readings of Carle's *The Grouchy Ladybug*, with all joining in on the refrain. There are exciting possibilities for bridging choric speaking into individual interpretations by using Moore's *See My Lovely Poison Ivy*. One poem from this collection, "Something Is There," works especially well if its lines are divided between two readers who take the parts of two children trying to scare each other, building up to a final line that shows genuine fright:

> Something is there
>   there on the stair
>   coming down
>   coming down
>   stepping with care.
>   Coming down
>   Coming down
>   slinkety-sly
>
> Something is coming and wants to get by.

From Lilian Moore. *See My Lovely Poison Ivy.* Illustrated by Diane Dawson. New York: Atheneum, 1979. Text copyright © 1972, 1975 Lilian Moore; illustrations copyright © 1975 Diane Dawson.

Individually, or paired or divided into groups of one-stanza-each, students enjoy the sing-along ease of two book-length poems from Children's Choices: Hoberman's *A House Is a House for Me* and Plath's *The Bed Book*. Both books may seem childish to sixth graders and above; yet, even at these levels, the challenge to perform the poems to entertain younger people arouses interest. In fact, almost any group responds to this invitation, "Let's put this poem on tape, send it to three second grades, and find out what they think of it."

A House Is a House for Me is more challenging than first appears. Rhythm dominates, but it is a rhythm that grows tiresome until we concentrate on the variety of images and the circus-like movement given to the reading. Ask readers to picture as explicitly as possible the dog-kennel-flea stanza as they read aloud: "A kennel's a house for a dog, dog./A dog is a house for a flea..." (from *A House Is a House for Me* by Mary Ann Hoberman. Illustrated by Betty Frasek. Text copyright © 1978 by Mary Ann Hoberman. Illustrations copyright © 1978 by Betty Frasek. Reprinted by permission of Viking Penguin, Inc.). Then contrast this reading with the expansive final stanza ending with "And the earth is a house for us all." Ask readers to try to figure out why the stanzas are arranged as they are. (For example, is there a change, as the poem moves along, in the kinds of houses it describes or in the poet's way of telling about them? Can the images and the arrangement be shown in the way you read the poem?)

The Bed Book's imagery is marvelously aided by McCully's watercolor illustrations, and the dreamy, floating excursions over the moonlit world set a mood that oral reading should reflect. The oral interpreter of this poem has an intricate but rewarding task: to display the richness of Plath's slant rhymes (*double, cradle, trundle*) and to highlight her contrasts in rhyme and imagery. One needs, for example, to display a forced, slower rhythm and pace for a "Submarine nosing through water" contrasted with a mechanical strong rhythm for:

A Tank Bed's got cranks
and wheels and cogs
and levers to pull
if you're stuck in bogs.

From *The Bed Book* by Sylvia Plath, illustrated by Emily Arnold McCully. Copyright © 1976 by Ted Hughes. Reprinted by permission of Harper & Row, Publishers, Inc.

Sebesta

Bringing serious poetry from print to oral interpretations is as difficult as playing music or basketball or solving a John le Carré mystery. It's an all-out activity. Readers must draw upon their schemata—patterns of past experiences and remembered emotions. They must use clues the poet, illustrator, and publisher have provided. You do not have to be struck by a tornado to effectively read aloud *Tornado!*, but you need to make the hookup between your own similar experience of crisis and that of the child-narrator in the poem. Adoff's broken staccato lines will help, as will the epilogue which presents an explicit prose account of what really happened. And Himler's somber illustrations—anxious faces that do not give way to panic—are perhaps the best clues of all. All of those images, remembrances, and clues can inspire a moving interpretation of this poem.

INSIDE THE HOUSE
inside
      the noise
we seem
      too small
for
the
     wild
     wind
     dark
     time
and
the
  clock has
      stopped
but
  it
  is
   tornado
    time

From Arnold Adoff. *Tornado! Poems.* Illustrated by Ronald Himler. Copyright Delacorte Press, 1976, 1977.

A few additional suggestions may aid interpretation. The value of each will depend on whether it applies to a specific poem.

2. Some poems are aided by actions and the suggestion of sound effects. In *Tornado!* the shriek of the approaching

storm or the ambulance siren can be played on a tape as background for the imagery conveyed by the speaker.

3. Poets work from many different points of view. Myra Cohn Livingston, a prolific poet represented on one Children's Choices list by her *The Way Things Are and Other Poems*, is adept at catching the speech patterns and diction of preadolescents. The rich collection of poems in *My Dad Is a Cool Dude*, by Karana Fufuka, seems to come from several distinct voices caught timelessly by the poet. With poems such as these, the reader can get a grip on interpretation by asking, "Who is the *speaker* in this poem?" Once a speaker is identified, the poem is read from that point of view. Further questions may also help: "What, exactly, is the situation in this poem? Why is it a poem? What has the poet done to show that the idea is important enough to be a poem?" Once these questions are clarified, readers are on their way to meaningful interpretation.

4. A good coach or director helps us see ourselves, pointing out the effect we are producing, and suggests (but does not dictate) how we might do better. The best coaches for oral interpretation are those who listen best. Discuss the role of coach or director. Demonstrate it or ask a professional director or speech coach to visit your classroom. Then let students take turns at the helm, coaching the poetry reading performance of a selected partner. If the reading is taped before and after the coaching session, both coach and pupil can examine the difference. Incidentally, this coaching suggestion leads to better poetry comprehension than any other teaching technique we know.

5. Music and art activities can enhance poetry. Have students select background music to set off a poem's tone and rhythm. Ask them to find or create a photograph or painting to provide a striking, illuminating match for a poem. But beware of the "blanket" assignment used indiscriminately. A cartoon may be fine for a limerick, a solid-color paper cut-out for a nursery rhyme; but neither is likely to serve the tone of a quiet lyric or character study. Form follows function in art projects as well as in architecture. An interesting project, gaining popularity in some places, is to transcribe a short poem into calligraphy (Eager, 1978)—certainly an exercise with intrinsic purpose, since it directs attention to the medium of the words themselves.

Sebesta

Enjoying Poetry

All of the above suggestions for selecting and interpreting poetry are intended to create active enjoyment. They are intended to help children and young people discover the "cool web of language that winds us in," as Graves put it, the manner in which language in its best form gives us a commonality of images to enrich our lives. The Children's Choices lists give us a good start in reaching for this goal. They assure us that children, too, are pursuing the goal. Our task is to help them.

Bibliography: Books of Poetry

Adoff, Arnold (Ed.). *My Black Me: A Beginning Book of Black Poetry*. New York: E.P. Dutton, 1974.

Adoff, Arnold. *Tornado! Poems*. Illustrated by Ronald Himler. New York: Delacorte, 1977.

Baylor, Byrd. *The Desert Is Theirs*. Illustrated by Peter Parnall. New York: Scribner's, 1975.

Bodecker, N.M. *Hurry, Hurry, Mary Dear! and Other Nonsense Poems*. New York: McElderry/Atheneum, 1976.

Carle, Eric. *The Grouchy Ladybug*. New York: Thomas Y. Crowell, 1977.

Frost, Robert. *Stopping by Woods on a Snowy Evening*. Illustrated by Susan Jeffers. New York: E.P. Dutton, 1978.

Fufuka, Karama. *My Dad Is a Cool Dude*. Illustrated by Mahiri Fufuka. New York: Dial, 1975.

Gardner, John. *A Child's Bestiary*. New York: Knopf, 1977.

Hoberman, Mary Ann. *A House Is a House for Me*. Illustrated by Betty Fraser. New York: Viking, 1978.

Kuskin, Karla. *Near the Window Tree*. New York: Harper & Row, 1975.

Lee, Dennis. *Alligator Pie*. Illustrated by Frank Newfield. Boston: Houghton Mifflin, 1974.

Livingston, Myra Cohn. *The Way Things Are and Other Poems*. New York: McElderry/Atheneum, 1974.

Lobel, Arnold (selected by). *Gregory Griggs and Other Nursery Rhyme People*. New York: Greenwillow, 1978.

Martin, Sarah Catherine. *Old Mother Hubbard and Her Dog*. Illustrated by Ib Spang Olsen. New York: Coward, McCann, & Geoghegan, 1976.

Moore, Lillian. *See My Lovely Poison Ivy*. Illustrated by Diane Dawson. New York: Atheneum, 1979.

Orgel, Doris. *Merry Merry FIBruary*. Illustrated by Arnold Lobel. New York: Parent's Magazine Press, 1977.

Plath, Sylvia. *The Bed Book*. Illustrated by Emily Arnold McCully. New York: Harper & Row, 1976.

Prelutsky, Jack. *The Mean Old Mean Hyena*. Illustrated by Arnold Lobel. New York: Greenwillow, 1978.

Riley, James Whitcomb. *An the Gobble-Uns'll Git You Ef You Don't Watch Out!* ("Little Orphant Annie"). Illustrated by Joel Schick. New York: Lippincott, 1975.

Worth, Valerie. *More Small Poems*. Illustrated by Natalie Babbitt. New York: Farrar, Straus & Giroux, 1976.

Zuromskis, Diane (Illustrator). *The Farmer in the Dell*. Boston: Little, Brown, 1978.

References

Ashley, L.F. *Children's Reading and the 1970s*. Toronto: McClelland & Stewart, 1972.

Eager, Fred. *Italic Handwriting for Young People*. New York: Collier Books, 1978.

Fisher, Carol J., & Natarella, Margaret A. "Of Cabbages and Kings: Or What Kinds of Poetry Young Children Like." *Language Arts*, 1979, *56*, 380-385.

Gullan, Marjorie. *Choral Speaking*. Boston: Expression Company, 1931.

Moray, Geraldine. "What Does Research Say About the Reading Interests of Children in the Intermediate Grades?" *Reading Teacher*, 1978, *31*, 763-768.

Nelson, Richard C. "Children's Poetry Preferences." *Elementary English*, 1966, *43*, 247-251.

Terry, Ann. *Children's Poetry Preferences: A National Survey of Upper Elementary Grades*. Urbana, Illinois: National Council of Teachers of English, 1974.

Tom, Chow Loy. "What Teachers Read to Pupils in the Middle Grades," unpublished dissertation, Ohio State University, 1969.

The Development of a Literature Program

Helen Huus
University of Missouri at Kansas City

A literate society requires that people be able to read and that they do read. The government support to school libraries in the 1960s stimulated the development of elementary school libraries but, more often than not, when budgets must be cut, libraries suffer. The decade of the 1970s saw Right to Read programs in the schools, but much of that emphasis was focused on teaching how to read. Remedial programs, reading materials, and computerized techniques were pointed toward learning how to read. Much less attention was paid to encouraging the literates to continue reading once they had learned.

Elementary school schedules regularly include class time devoted specifically to the teaching of reading. Some states mandate the minimum time that must be spent for each grade. Not so with exposure to literature—reading the best of prose and poetry. True, secondary schools do have separate literature courses, but rarely are such courses found in elementary schools. In addition, some states do not require elementary school teachers to take a course in literature for children as part of their teacher preparation. So, it is no wonder literature is slighted at the lower educational levels.

The Missouri Commissioner of Education, Arthur L. Mallory, and other educators across the state were concerned about the need to develop permanent readers among elementary school children and to help the children become acquainted with good literature. As a result, Director of Curriculum Grace McReynolds was requested to prepare a curriculum guide for children's literature to be used from kindergarten through grade eight.

As a first step, letters were sent to all fifty states, requesting copies of their current guides for children's literature. Only one state submitted a guide (along with a note of apology for its being so out of date).

Next, a consultant prepared the first tentative draft of a guide. At the start, in-house discussions were held with various curriculum specialists in the Department of Elementary and Secondary Education regarding the content and organization of the guide. Eventually, an organization evolved that included the following: objectives; criteria for book selection and evaluation of pupils' learning; suggestions for teaching, including sample lesson plans; a graded and categorized list of books; suggestions for ways parents can help; a listing of Mark Twain Awards, Missouri authors, and poets for children; a bibliography; and acknowlegements.

Objectives of the Program

The objectives of the literature program were derived from sources such as the Nebraska Curriculum for Literature, the teacher's manual for the Field Literature Series, textbooks for children's literature courses, and discussions with experts. The following five objectives were selected: 1) To enjoy reading and to develop the habit of reading good books; 2) to develop literary awareness; 3) to use literature in understanding oneself and others; 4) to think critically and respond creatively to literature; and 5) to evaluate personal reading and extend literary appreciation.

Selection Criteria

Criteria were set up to aid in the selection of the prose and poetry for the guide, and also to aid teachers who would use the guide in selecting books on their own. At all times, the literary value of the books was kept foremost. The elements of literature considered in the selection were the same as used for evaluating literature for adults, while recognizing the difference in the maturity level of the audience. These elements included theme; setting; plot; characterization; point of view; style; and, especially for picture books, format and illustration.

Theme is the overarching idea, the universal qualities exemplified by the story. Books selected for the guide contained themes of courage, loyalty, friendship, security, perseverance, and right triumphing over wrong—all positive attributes that contribute to the development of one's character. Some themes

Huus

show the resilience of children facing problems of growing up and coming to terms with themselves.

The specific setting for some books is irrelevant to the story, but Holling's *Paddle to the Sea*, for example, could have happened only along the Great Lakes and the St. Lawrence River, as the "paddle person"—the small, carved Indian in his canoe—follows the currents to the ocean. Likewise, the details of everyday living in Laura Ingalls Wilder's books are specific to frontier life in the American Middle West and essential to the stories.

Of course, every good story has a plot, but sometimes it is subordinate to other literary elements. In folk/fairy tales, however, plot is paramount. The problem is set, the action quickly moves forward to a successful solution, and everyone "lives happily ever after." Plots containing danger, suspense, and conflict keep readers interested to the very end, and books for the young usually finish with a satisfying resolution or at least on a note of hope.

Characters—whether people, animals, or imaginary creatures—must be believable and consistent in their actions. Charlotte in *Charlotte's Web* is a spider, but E.B. White's masterful treatment makes her a wonderful spiderperson indeed. And Paddington Bear, though stuffed to be sure, creates havoc such as only a living, breathing creature could. The list of human characters among the classics must include Heidi, Jo, Tom and Huck, and Hans, and modern fiction adds others each year.

Most stories for young people are told from the storyteller's point of view in the third person. Occasionally, first person is used, as in the Henry Reed stories by Robertson, which are actually the journals Henry kept. *Time of Wonder* by McCloskey is one of the few books written in the second person—"you" are there.

Style is one of the distinguishing features of literature— the vocabulary, syntax, cadence, and figures of speech that lift the writing above the mediocre. Phrases like Kipling's "great, grey-green, greasy, Limpopo River," from *The Elephant's Child*, or Winnie-the-Pooh's "Sustaining Book," such as would "help and comfort a Wedged Bear in Great Tightness" are remembered and cherished long after the book has been put away.

While illustrations enhance almost any text, they are an essential element in picture books. Gag's *Millions of Cats* and Sendak's *Where the Wild Things Are* provide such an integration of picture and story that it is inconceivable to think of one without the other. Artists of note have helped create books for children that are among the most beautiful in the world and readers absorb, sometimes unconsciously, an artistic standard through their experiences with fine books.

For poetry, elements of rhythm, rhyme, sound patterns, imagery, mood, and form were considered in setting criteria for selection. A child's first exposure to poetry is often the rhythm of the Mother Goose rhyme "Pat-a-Cake," as doting adults clap the baby's hands in time. One familiar rhyme scheme has second and fourth lines rhyming, as in "Mary, Mary, Quite Contrary." Unusual rhyme schemes are also found, as in Armour's "Money," which begins "Workers earn it/Spend-thrifts burn it." Sounds and images are exemplified in Brown's "Bumble Bee," where the bee is described as a "Rumbly/Tumbly/Bumbly Bee," while "Someone" by de la Mare leaves a haunting question as the poem ends: "So I know not who came knocking/At all, at all, at all." As to form, Behn's *Cricket Songs* are haiku translated from the Japanese; other poems suitable for children include ballads and narrative works. In all, poetry for children represents a wide variety of form and style, and the selections for the guide recognized this fact.

Suggestions for Teaching

Teaching literature is not peculiarly different from any other teaching as such, in that objectives are stated, activities to achieve the objectives are conducted, and an evaluation is carried out to determine whether objectives have been achieved. Nevertheless, within this general frame of reference, some specific suggestions for literature teaching seemed appropriate for the developing guide. Therefore, a section entitled "Teaching Literature in the Elementary School" was included, giving ideas for creating a reading environment and for organizing the class. Since only one copy of a work was likely to be available, it was assumed that much of the teaching would be done orally and with the class as a whole, but suggestions for group and individual activities also were presented. Examples of types of accompanying questions—literal, interpretive, evaluative, reactive, integrative, and creative—were explained, and ways of evaluating each objective was presented.

One section of the guide titled "Planning the Literature Lessons" included possibilities for introducing lessons, conducting discussions, carrying out related activities, and evaluating responses. A list of useful materials for creative activities was given, but emphasis was constantly placed on the books as literature, that is, as beautiful language and thought, so that activities would enhance rather than usurp the literature experience.

Sample teaching plans for six lessons were prepared, one each of prose and poetry for primary, middle grade, and upper levels. The selections chosen were: *The Courage of Sarah Nobel* by Alice Dalgliesh and "Snow in the City" by Rachel Field; *The Cricket in Times Square* by George Selden and "Jabberwocky" by Lewis Carroll; *Have Space Suit, Will Travel* by Robert Heinlein and "Foul Shot" by Edwin A. Hoey. Since the prose selections were too long to be read aloud at one sitting, the books were divided into logical parts for presentation.

A graded reading list was compiled, arranged by months from September to May. In making selections, sources such as the following were consulted:

- Newbery, Caldecott, and Mark Twain Award lists
- American Library Association's annual lists of Notable Books
- *School Library Journal*'s annual Best Books of the Year
- Lists of children's classics
- *Bound-to-Stay-Bound Books, K-12*
- Bibliographies in textbooks for children's literature classes
- Virginia Haviland's annual *Children's Books*
- Robert Carlsen's *Books and the Teen Age Reader*.

Grade placements were established more by concept level than by reading level, recognizing that most of the selections (especially at lower levels) would be read aloud. Assignment to a given month was done by topic where appropriate (e.g., Halloween stories and poems for October) but beyond that, an attempt was made to provide a variety of genre and topics for each month. This monthly arrangement was used for kindergarten through grade five; for grades six through eight, books and poems were listed in categories only, partly because books for these ages are longer and partly because these students are probably reading more books on their own. The categories used throughout the guide were: Folk/Fairy Tales; Myths, Fables, Heroes; Historical, Holidays; Fantasy, Nonsense; Other Lands; Animals, Plants; Biography; Weather, Seasons, Earth; Information, Miscellaneous; Modern; and Poetry. Obviously, a book could be classified under more than one category, and placements were made rather arbitrarily.

Evaluation, Publication, and Distribution

The original listing of books was screened by three committees, their members selected throughout the state. First, a committee of children's literature specialists, including teachers of children's literature in colleges and universities and children's librarians from public libraries, reviewed the list for literary merit and made suggestions for additions and deletions. Second, a committee of educators, including school librarians and classroom teachers in elementary and junior high schools, reviewed the list primarily to evaluate the placement of books by grade and month but also to suggest additions and deletions. Third, a committee of administrators and citizens (superintendents, principals, business persons, presidents of parent-teacher organizations, library board members, and interested citizens) met and made suggestions, emphasizing classical books, informational books, and books for family reading. After each committee met, the list was revised, incorporating the suggestions where possible, and then the next committee received the revised list for consideration. The first two committees received the list approximately one week prior to their meeting but, because of time pressure, this was not possible for the third committee.

Books on the list were then read by a committee including librarians, retired teachers, and teachers on leave in order to evaluate not only literary quality but vocabulary and ethics, so that the books on the list also met standards of good taste.

The final draft of the guide was then prepared and sent to the State Publications Committee for their comments. After final editing and layout were completed, bids were let, and eventually the finished product, *A Guide for Children's Literature, K-8*, appeared in August 1980.

Complimentary copies were sent to the chief school officer in each of the fifty states and to all elementary and junior high schools in Missouri. One copy was made available without cost for every ten teachers at these two levels in the state, but additional copies could be purchased at cost.

Implementation

Once the *Guide* became available, the next step was implementation; i.e., seeing that the classroom teachers were familiar with and could use the publication. Consequently, in Fall 1980, a series of eleven workshops were held, one for each of the educational districts in the state, with administrators and representative teachers from each school invited to attend. The *Guide* was presented, a demonstration lesson incorporating ideas from the *Guide* was given, and questions were answered.

The "proof of the pudding" still remains. We hope teachers and librarians are using the *Guide* and adding their own ideas so that the lives of the students will be enriched by literature and that pleasant experiences with good books will help make these students lifelong readers.

Bibliography

Behn, Henry (translator). *Cricket Songs*. New York: Harcourt Brace Jovanovich, 1964.
Dalgliesh, Alice. *The Courage of Sarah Noble*. Illustrated by Leonard Weisgard. New York: Scribner's, 1954.
Gag, Wanda. *Millions of Cats*. New York: Coward, McCann & Geoghegan, 1928.
Heinlein, Robert. *Have Space Suit, Will Travel*. New York: Scribner's, 1977.
Holling, Holling Clancy. *Paddle to the Sea*. Boston: Houghton Mifflin, 1941.
Kipling, Rudyard. *The Elephant's Child*. Illustrated by Leonard Weisgard. New York: Walker, 1970.
McCloskey, Robert. *Time of Wonder*. New York: Viking, 1957.
Selden, George. *Cricket in Times Square*. Illustrated by Garth Williams. New York: Farrar, Straus & Giroux, 1976.
Sendak, Maurice. *Where the Wild Things Are*. New York: Harper & Row, 1963.
White, E.B. *Charlotte's Web*. Illustrated by Garth Williams. New York: Harper & Row, 1952.

References

"Best Books of the Year," December issues of the *School Library Journal.*

Book Evaluation Committee. "Notable Children's Books." Annual editions, Chicago: American Library Association.

Bound-to-Stay-Bound Books, K-12. Annual editions. Jacksonville, Illinois: Bound-to-Stay-Bound, Inc.

Carlsen, Robert. *Books and the Teen Age Reader.* New York: Harper & Row, 1967. Also Bantam Books.

A Guide to Children's Literature, K-8. Jefferson City, Missouri: Missouri Department of Elementary and Secondary Education, 1980.

Haviland, Virginia (Compiler). *Children's Books: A List of Books for Preschool through Junior High School Age.* Annual editions. Washington, D.C.: Superintendent of Documents, Government Printing Office.

Huus, Helen, et al. (Compiler). *Field Literature Series, K-8.* Reading, Massachusetts: Addison-Wesley, 1971.

Selecting Trade Books with Children

Helene Lang
University of Vermont

We know children read to learn and to enjoy. We know some children learn to read easily and for others reading prowess is achieved by a more difficult route. By whatever means teachers and parents help children toward learning and enjoyment, there is need for exposure to and involvement with good books. Books are the means for children to relate learning to read to their lives. When books are made available to children, they seek books. Their reading improves. They explore the world in an infinite variety of ways—seeking, seeing, thinking, and feeling.

Criteria for Selection

There is no one set of standards that when met automatically ensures that a book is of immediate or lasting value. Stewig (1980) tells us that the appellation "good" is a fragile raft of opinion resting precariously on the shifting quicksand of taste. But there are accepted ways to look at and judge books to be used in classrooms.

First, consider the plot carefully. Is it orderly and presented in a good tempo? Children tend to abandon books in which the plot drags and they are forced to wait for something to happen. Action must be immediate.

Characters should be honest and credibly consistent. Believable characters have weaknesses as well as strengths and need to be portrayed "in the round," rather than in flat stereotypes. Growth or change in the character needs to be in keeping with earlier development.

Themes for good children's books should nourish the mind and the emotions of the readers. Worthy ideas presented through literature transmit attitudes and contribute to the reader's developing value system.

A fourth consideration in trade book selection is that of setting. Settings in contemporary books are frequently more psychological than social. Yet, both types of settings are worthy, with one at times enhancing the other. One such example is Paterson's *Jacob Have I Loved*. This book's setting weaves knowledge of the Chesapeake Bay with the psychological setting of the rivalry of twins.

Style of writing helps children to learn about written language and can contribute to the book's readability. Style is the manner in which the author uses language to clothe ideas. It influences comfortable movement through print. Style may be the clipped language of humor so generously used by Danziger, or the dialogue in books by Blume or Cleary. Style is the author's indelible stamp on the message.

While no one can be absolutely certain of the influence of a book's illustrations on children's reactions, I believe that illustrations in children's books should support the text, and delight the eyes and heart. They should inform the reader of worlds real and imaginary. Good illustrations present true feelings without sentimentality.

Vocabulary load and, hence, the concept load are important considerations. We have long since abandoned bland vocabulary limits for trade books. It is rich language well used that increases reading ability—by stretching the mind and helping to develop ideas.

Print size and style, spacing, balance on the page, and even the size of the book itself—all contribute to relative ease of reading.

For books of information, scope and sequence should be considered in selection. Books should cover what they purport to cover. They should provide a clear sequence which helps make the content clear.

Conclusions

To use trade books effectively, teachers must resolve to read aloud daily to their children. And to that age-old maxim, we should add: Teachers should read well and show their own enjoyment in books. By first selecting books wisely and then sharing them well, we take one giant step toward making good readers: We entice with books. In addition, we are offering the language of books, which is different from oral language. We are helping young readers to form a base for judgments and predictions about story structure and style.

Second, trade books are logical vehicles for extending reading. Teachers use them to provide a link with classroom materials and units of study. They form the base for responding in a variety of modes.

Third, our use of trade books within classrooms means that instructional time must come from somewhere. Using trade books may mean less time for skills and perhaps that is as it should be.

I suggest making use of the variety of selection aids available to teachers—including those of our professional organizations, and of established reviewing tools such as the *Bulletin of the Center for Children's Books* (University of Chicago). I further recommend wide reading of children's books and the cultivation of a knowledgeable librarian—all of which contribute to wiser selections. Most of all, learn to guide and trust children's judgments about books, such as the offerings of the Children's Choices lists. And then—read.

References

Paterson, Katherine. *Jacob Have I Loved*. New York: Thomas Y. Crowell, 1980.

Stewig, John. *Children and Literature*. Chicago: Rand McNally, 1980.

Reading Interest Research and Children's Choices

M. Jean Greenlaw
North Texas State University

During the first six years that children voiced their preferences for current children's books and those preferences were compiled into the Children's Choices List, nearly 700 titles emerged. Using categories that my colleague and I had determined through earlier research, I categorized and ranked the types of books children selected through the Children's Choices project. I was then able to inspect these rankings and compare them with types of books students preferred in the earlier study (Greenlaw & Moore).

The data from the original study were based on 1,690 students (450 primary; 1,240 intermediate) equally divided by sex. Nearly 10,000 readers are represented in the Children's Choices List tabulations.

Results for Primary Level Books

Of the 374 primary level books selected, those classified as *funny* were a distinct first place choice. Ninety-six books (or 26 percent) fit that category. Books designated *make-believe*, about *people*, and *animal stories* were in second place; *real things, rhyme*, and *mystery* comprised a third group; and *fairytales, sports*, and *how-to-do-it* books were among the fewest chosen.

Results for Upper Level Books

Books selected that were appropriate for upper level reading (N = 306) were also categorized by type. *Adventure, jokes/humor*, and *informational* books were the first levels of choice; *fantasy, mystery, sports*, and the *supernatural* were in second place; *how-to-do-it, biography, historical fiction*, and *poetry* were in the third level; and *science fiction* and *romance* were least chosen.

Table 1   Summary of Primary Grade Category Selections

Children's Choices Story Type	Total #	Sample %	Research Rankings Story Type
Funny	96	26	Funny
Make-Believe	72	19	Mysteries
People	66	18	Sports
Animals	43	12	Animals
Real Things	29	8	Fairy Tales
Rhyme	23	6	How-to-Do-It
Mysteries	20	5	Rhyme
Fairy Tales	12	3	Real Things
Sports	9	2	Make-Believe
How-to-Do-It	4	1	People
Total	374	100%	

Table 2   Summary of Upper Grade Category Selections

Children's Choices Genre	Total #	Sample %	Research Rankings Genre
Adventure	64	21	Mystery
Jokes/Humor	54	18	Adventure
Informational	47	15	Science Fiction
Fantasy	30	10	Sports
Mystery	22	7	Romance
Sports	21	7	Jokes/Humor
Supernatural	19	6	Fantasy
How-to-Do-It	12	4	Informational
Biography	12	4	Supernatural
Historical Fiction	10	3	How-to-Do-It
Poetry	9	3	Biography
Science Fiction	4	1	Historical Fiction
Romance	2	1	Poetry
Total	306	100%	

Discussion

By comparing the columns on the two tables, one can see that the Children's Choices list is reflective of data gathered in systematic research. Children's Choices lists, then, seem to represent reasonable book selection aids for use by teachers, parents, and librarians.

When discrepancies exist—for example, the categories of *mystery* and *sports* were high on the list of stated preferences, but low on actual number of books selected for Children's Choices—the differences may be attributable to the number of books available in these categories for primary age children. The converse might be true when considering the categories *make-believe* and *people*. Large numbers of books are available that represent these categories, and though children don't consider them high on their stated categories of preference, they can discover many books they do like that fit these categories.

Discrepancies that exist for the upper level books may be similarly explained, i.e., the number of books published in a particular year affects the sample in the Children's Choices project. When fewer books are published in a particular category, it follows that the category will be disproportionately represented on a final tally.

Bibliography

Greenlaw, M. Jean, & Moore, David M. Research in Students' Reading Interests: Grades 1-12 (manuscript).

Greenlaw, M. Jean, & Wielan, O. Paul. Reading Interests Revisited, *Language Arts*, 1979, *56*, 432-434.

Norvell, George W. *The Reading Interests of Young People*. Boston: D.C. Heath, 1950.

Robinson, Helen M., & Weintraub, Sam. "Research Related to Children's Interests and to Developmental Values of Reading," *Library Trends*, 1973, *22*, 81-108.

Terman, Lewis M., & Lima, Margaret. *Children's Reading*. New York: Appleton-Century, 1925, 1935.

True, M.B.C. "What My Pupils Read," *Education*, 1889, *10*, 42-45.

Weintraub, Sam. "Two Significant Trends in Reading Research." In H. Alan Robinson (Ed.), *Reading and Writing Instruction in the United States: Historical Trends*. Newark, Delaware: International Reading Association, 1977.

Children's Choices: A Composite Bibliography

The following bibliography represents a composite listing of seven years of children's favorite books, as determined by the Children's Choices selection procedures. Each year, since its initiation, the list has appeared in either the October or November issues of *The Reading Teacher*. As a service to teachers, librarians, parents, and other selectors of children's books, the lists are compiled here. Users should note that the books are arranged as they are in their original formats under the following headings:

> Beginning Independent Reading
> Younger Readers
> Middle Grades
> Older Readers
> Informational Books
> Poetry/Verse

The date in parentheses in each entry refers to the year in which that book appeared on the Children's Choices List, rather than its year of publication. The year of publication is typically the year *prior* to a book's selection, except for the first two years, 1974 and 1975. Users can also determine that a book is currently available in paperback (P) and if an edition is out of print (O/P).

Beginning Independent Reading

Amy for Short. Laura Joffe Numeroff. Macmillan. 48 pp. (1977).

Animals Should Definitely Not Act Like People. Judi Barrett. Ill. by Ron Barrett. Atheneum. 30 pp. (1981).

The Animals Who Changed Their Colors. Pascale Allamand. Ill. by the author. Lothrop. 32 pp. (1980).

Arthur's Eyes. Marc Brown. Ill. by the author. Atlantic-Little, Brown. 32 pp. (1980). P, Avon.

Arthur's Pen Pal. Lillian Hoban. Ill. by the author. Harper. 64 pp. (1977). P, Xerox.

Arthur's Prize Reader. Lillian Hoban. Ill. by the author. Harper. 64 pp. (1979). P, Harper.

The Bean Boy. Joan Chase Bowden. Ill. by Sal Murdocca. Macmillan. 62 pp. (1980).

Bear Hunt. Anthony Browne. Ill. by the author. Atheneum. 24 pp. (1981).

Benjamin's Dreadful Dream. Alan Baker. Ill. by the author. Lippincott. 32 pp. (1981).

Birth of a Foal. Jane Miller. Photographs by the author. Lippincott. 44 pp. (1978). P, Scholastic.

Bony. Frances Zweifel. Ill. by Whitney Darrow, Jr. Harper. 64 pp. (1978).

Boo! Bernard Most. Ill. by the author. Prentice. 32 pp. (1981).

Bullfrog and Gertrude Go Camping. Rosamond Dauer. Ill. by Byron Barton. Greenwillow. 40 pp. (1981).

Bullfrog Grows Up. Rosamond Dauer. Ill. by Byron Barton. Greenwillow. 56 pp. (1977).

But No Elephants. Jerry Smath. Ill. by the author. Parents. 42 pp. (1980).

Cat at Bat. John Stadler. Ill. by the author. Dutton. 32 pp. (1980).

Chameleon Was a Spy. Diane Redfield Massie. Ill. by the author. Crowell. 40 pp. (1980).

Detective Mole. Robert Quackenbush. Ill. by the author. Lothrop. 63 pp. (1977).

Double-Decker, Double-Decker, Double-Decker Bus. Patty Wolcott. Ill. by Bob Barner. Addison. 24 pp. (1981).

Eliza's Daddy. Ianthe Thomas. Ill. by Moneta Barnett. Harcourt. 64 pp. (1977). P. Harcourt.

Everyone Ready? Franz Brandenberg. Ill. by Aliki. Greenwillow. 55 pp. (1980).

The Farmer in the Dell. Diane Zuromskis. Ill. by the author. Little, Brown. 32 pp. (1979).

The First Morning. Margery Bernstein and Janet Kobrin. Ill. by Enid Warner Romanek. Scribner's. 44 pp. (1977).

First Pink Light. Eloise Greenfield. Ill. by Moneta Barnett. Crowell. 36 pp. (1977).

Fish Story. Robert Tallon. Ill. by the author. Holt. 27 pp. (1978). P, Scholastic.

Freight Train. Donald Crews. Ill. by the author. Greenwillow. 24 pp. (1979).

Frog and Toad All Year. Arnold Lobel. Ill. by the author. Harper. 64 pp. (1977).

Frog Goes to Dinner. Mercer Mayer. Ill. by the author. Dial. 32 pp. (1974). P, Dial.

George and Martha Tons of Fun. James Marshall. Ill. by the author. Houghton. 48 pp. (1981).

Good Morning, Chick. Mirra Ginsburg. Ill. by Byron Barton. Greenwillow. 32 pp. (1981).

Grasshopper on the Road. Arnold Lobel. Ill. by the author. Harper. 64 pp. (1979). P, Harper.

The Great Thumbprint Drawing Book. Ed Emberley. Ill. by the author. Little, Brown. 37 pp. (1978).

Hand Talk: An ABC of Finger Spelling & Sign Language. Remy Charlip, Mary Beth Ancona, and George Ancona. Four Winds. 46 pp. (1974).

Harry and Shelburt. Dorothy O. Van Woerkom. Ill. by Erick Ingraham. Macmillan. 48 pp. (1978).

Honk Honk! Anne Rockwell. Ill. by the author. Dutton. 32 pp. (1981).

Humphrey the Dancing Pig. Arthur Getz. Ill. by the author. Dial. 32 pp. (1981). P, Dial.

If the Dinosaurs Came Back. Bernard Most. Ill. by the author. Harcourt. 32 pp. (1979).

Ig Lives in a Cave. Carol Chapman. Ill. by Bruce Degen. Dutton. 56 pp. (1980).

Is It Red? Is It Yellow? Is It Blue? Tana Hoban. Photographs by the author. Greenwillow. 32 pp. (1979).

Jenny and the Tennis Nut. Janet Schulman. Ill. by Marilyn Hafner. Greenwillow. 56 pp. (1979). P, Dell.

Lambs for Dinner. Betsy Maestro. Ill. by Giulio Maestro. Crown. 32 pp. (1979).

The Last Puppy. Frank Asch. Ill. by the author. Prentice. 32 pp. (1981).

Little Otter Remembers. Ann Tombert. Ill. by John Wallner. Crown. 64 pp. (1978).

The Littlest Leaguer. Syd Hoff. Ill. by the author. Windmill. 48 pp. (1977). P, Windmill.

Lost in the Museum. Miriam Cohen. Ill. by Lillian Hoban. Greenwillow. 32 pp. (1980).

Matilda Hippo Has a Big Mouth. Dennis Panek. Ill. by the author. Bradbury. 32 pp. (1981).

May I Visit? Charlotte Zolotow. Ill. by Erik Blegvad. Harper. 32 pp. (1977).

Mildred and the Mummy. Lady McCrady. Ill. by the author. Holiday. 32 pp. (1981).

Mine Will, Said John. Helen V. Griffith. Ill. by Muriel Batherman. Greenwillow. 32 pp. (1981).

Mr. Miller The Dog. Helme Heine. Ill. by the author. McElderry/Atheneum. 64 pp. (1981).

Mooch the Messy. Marjorie Weinman Sharmat. Ill. by Ben Shecter. Harper. 64 pp. (1977).

Morris Has a Cold. Bernard Wiseman. Ill. by the author. Dodd. 48 pp. (1979). P, Scholastic.

Mother Rabbit's Son Tom. Dick Gackenbach. Ill. by the author. Harper. 32 pp. (1978).

Mouse Soup. Arnold Lobel. Ill. by the author. Harper. 64 pp. (1978).

The Mystery of the Flying Orange Pumpkin. Steve Kellogg. Ill. by the author. Dial. 32 pp. (1981).

Nate the Great and the Phony Clue. Marjorie Weinman Sharmat. Ill. by Marc Simont. Coward. 48 pp. (1978). P, Dell.

Naughty Nancy. John S. Goodall. Ill. by the author. Atheneum/McElderry. 32 pp. (1975).

The Night before Christmas. Clement Moore. Ill. by Tomie de Paola. Holiday. 32 pp. (1981). P, Holiday.

Nine at Carnival. Errol Lloyd. Ill. by the author. Crowell. 26 pp. (1980).

Oh, Were They Ever Happy! Peter Spier. Ill. by the author. Doubleday. 40 pp. (1979).

One Little Kitten. Tana Hoban. Photographs by the author. Greenwillow. 24 pp. (1980). P, Scholastic.

Oops. Mercer Mayer. Dial. 30 pp. (1978). P, Dial.

Ottie and the Star. Laura Jean Allen. Ill. by the author. Harper. 32 pp. (1980).

Penny-Wise, Fun-Foolish. Judy Delton. Ill. by Giulio Maestro. Crown. 48 pp. (1978).

Poofy Loves Company. Nancy Winslow Parker. Ill. by the author. Dodd. 32 pp. (1981).

Positively No Pets Allowed. Nathan Zimelman. Ill. by Pamela Johnson. Dutton. 32 pp. (1981).

Q is for Duck: An Alphabet Guessing Game. Mary Elting and Michael Folsom. Ill. by Jack Kent. Clarion/Houghton. 64 pp. (1981). P, Clarion/Houghton.

Samuel's Tree House. Bethany Tudor. Ill. by the author. Philomel. 28 pp. (1980).

Scarlet Monster Lives Here. Marjorie Weinman Sharmat. Ill. by Dennis Kendrick. Harper. 64 pp. (1980).

The Shopping Basket. John Burningham. Ill. by the author. Crowell. 32 pp. (1981).

Snake In, Snake Out. Linda Banchek. Ill. by Elaine Arnold. Crowell. 29 pp. (1979).

Some Swell Pup or Are you Sure You Want a Dog? Maurice Sendak and Matthew Margolis. Ill. by Maurice Sendak. Farrar. 26 pp. (1977). P, Puffin.

Space Case. Edward Marshall. Ill. by James Marshall. Dial. 40 pp. (1981).

Strong John. Joan Chase Bowden. Ill. by Sal Murdocca. Macmillan. 64 pp. (1981).

Super Bowl. Leonard Kessler. Ill. by the author. Greenwillow. 56 pp. (1981).

The Surprise Party. Annabelle Prager. Ill. by Tomie de Paola. Pantheon. 44 pp. (1978).

Ten Copycats in a Boat and Other Riddles. Alvin Schwartz. Ill. by Marc Simont. Harper. 64 pp. (1981).

Tony Dorsett. S.H. Buchard. Harcourt. 64 pp. (1979).

The Trip and Other Sophie and Gussie Stories. Marjorie Weinman Sharmat. Ill. by Lillian Hoban. Macmillan. 64 pp. (1977).

Two Is Company. Judy Delton. Ill. by Giulio Maestro. Crown. 47 pp. (1977).

UFO Kidnap! Nancy Robinson. Ill. by Edward Franklin. Lothrop. 63 pp. (1979).

Ugbu. Ora Ayal. Ill. by the author. Trans. from the Hebrew by Naomi Low Nakao. Harper. 32 pp. (1980).

Uproar on Hollercat Hill. Jean Marzollo. Ill. by Steven Kellogg. Dial. 32 pp. (1981).

We're in Big Trouble, Blackboard Bear. Martha Alexander. Ill. by the author. Dial. 32 pp. (1981).

What a Good Lunch! Shigeo Watanabe. Ill. by Yasuo Ohtomo. Philomel. 32 pp. (1981).

What's Inside the Box? Ethel Kessler and Leonard Kessler. Ill. by Leonard Kessler. Dodd. 48 pp. (1977).

Where Does the Teacher Live? Paula Kurzband Feder. Ill. by Lillian Hoban. Dutton. 48 pp. (1980).

Who's Afraid of the Dark? Crosby Bonsall. Ill. by the author. Harper. 32 pp. (1981).

Whose Birthday Is It? Bill Woodman. Ill. by the author. Crowell. 48 pp. (1981).

Witch, Goblin, and Sometimes Ghost: Six Read-Alone Stories. Sue Alexander. Ill. by Jeanette Winter. Pantheon. 61 pp. (1977).

Witches Four. Marc Brown. Ill. by the author. Parents. 40 pp. (1981).

Younger Readers

ABC of Monsters. Deborah Niland. Ill. by the author. McGraw. 30 pp. (1979).

Albert's Story. Claudia Long. Ill. by Judy Glasser. Delacorte. 32 pp. (1979).

Albert's Toothache. Barbara Williams. Ill. by Kay Chorao. Dutton. 32 pp. (1974). P, Dutton.

Alexander, Who Used to Be Rich Last Sunday. Judith Viorst. Ill. by Ray Cruz. Atheneum. 29 pp. (1979), P, Atheneum.

Amanda and the Giggling Ghost. Steven Kroll. Ill. by Dick Gackenbach. Holiday. 40 pp. (1981).

Amifika. Lucille Clifton. Ill. by Thomas DiGrazia. Dutton. 28 pp. (1978).

Amy's Dinosaur. Sid Hoff. Ill. by the author. Windmill. 48 pp. (1974). P, Windmill.

And I Mean It, Stanley. Crosby Bonsall. Ill. by the author. Harper. 32 pp. (1974).

Annie's Rainbow. Ron Brooks. Ill. by the author. Philomel. 28 pp. (1977).

Anybody Home? Aileen Fisher. Ill. by Susan Bonners. Crowell. 32 pp. (1981).

Appelard and Liverwurst. Mercer Mayer. Ill. by Steven Kellogg. Four Winds. 34 pp. (1979).

Apple Pigs. Ruth Orbach. Ill. by the author. Philomel. 32 pp. (1978).

Arion and the Dolphins. Lonzo Anderson. Ill. by Adrienne Adams. Scribner. 32 pp. (1979).

Arrow to the Sun: A Pueblo Indian Tale. Adapted and ill. by Gerald McDermott. Viking. 42 pp. (1974). P, Puffin.

Arthur's Nose. Marc Brown. Ill. by the author. Atlantic-Little, Brown. 31 pp. (1977). P, Avon.

Arthur's Valentine. Marc Brown. Ill. by the author. Atlantic-Little, Brown. 32 pp. (1981).

Bah! Humbug? Lorna Balian. Ill. by the author. Abingdon. 32 pp. (1978).

Barney Bipple's Magic Dandelions. Carol Chapman. Ill. by Steven Kellogg. Dutton. 27 pp. (1978).

Beany. Jane Feder. Ill. by Karen Gundersheimer. Pantheon. 32 pp. (1980).

The Bear and the Fly. Paula Winter. Crown. 32 pp. (1977). P, Scholastic.

Bear by Himself. Geoffrey Hayes. Ill. by the author. Harper. 32 pp. (1977).

The Bear on the Doorstep. Jane Flory, Ill. by Carolyn Croll. Houghton. 32 pp. (1981).

The Bear's Bicycle. Emilie Warren McLeod. Ill. by David McPhail. Atlantic-Little, Brown. 32 pp. (1975). P, Puffin.

The Bearskinner. Brothers Grimm. Ill. by Felix Hoffmann. McElderry/ Atheneum. 32 pp. (1979).

Bearymore. Don Freeman. Ill. by the author. Viking. 36 pp. (1977). P, Puffin.

The Berenstain Bears and the Missing Dinosaur Bone. Stan and Jan Berenstain. Ill. by the authors. Random. 48 pp. (1981). P, Random.

Bert and Barney. Ned Delaney. Ill. by the author. Houghton. 32 pp. (1980).

Big Bad Bruce. Bill Peet. Ill. by the author. Houghton. 38 pp. (1978).

A Big Fat Enormous Lie. Marjorie Weinman Sharmat. Ill. by David McPhail. Dutton. 30 pp. (1979).

Bill and Pete. Tomie de Paola. Ill. by the author. Putnam. 28 pp. (1979). P, Putnam.

The Birthday Trombone. Margaret A. Hartelius. Doubleday. 45 pp. (1978).

A Birthday Wish. Ed Emberley. Little, Brown. 32 pp. (1978).

Bonzo Beaver. Arthur Crowley. Ill. by Annie Gusman. Houghton. 32 pp. (1981). P, Houghton.

Boris and the Monsters. Elaine Macmann Willoughby. Ill. by Lynn Munsinger. Houghton. 32 pp. (1981).

The Bravest Babysitter. Barbara Greenberg. Ill. by Diane Paterson. Dial. 28 pp. (1978).

Bumps in the Night. Harry Allard. Ill. by James Marshall. Doubleday. 32 pp. (1980).

Burnie's Hill. Traditional rhyme ill. by Erik Blegvad. McElderry/Atheneum. 24 pp. (1978).

Bus Ride. Nancy Jewell. Ill. by Ronald Himler. Harper. 32 pp. (1979).

The Butterfly. A. Delaney. Ill. by the author. Delacorte. 27 pp. (1978).

Carrot Cake. Nonny Hogrogian. Ill. by the author. Greenwillow. 27 pp. (1978).

Catastrophe Cat. Dennis Panek. Ill. by the author. Bradbury. 31 pp. (1979).

Catastrophe Cat at the Zoo. Dennis Panek. Ill. by the author. Bradbury. 34 pp. (1980).

Chasing the Goblins Away. Tobi Tobias. Ill. by Victor Ambrus. Warne. 32 pp. (1978).

Chester Chipmunk's Thanksgiving. Barbara Williams. Ill. by Kay Chorao.
Dutton. 32 pp. (1979).

The Chicken's Child. Margaret A. Hartelius. Ill. by the author. Doubleday.
40 pp. (1975). P, Scholastic.

Circus. Jack Prelutsky. Ill. by Arnold Lobel. Macmillan. 32 pp. (1974). P,
Macmillan.

The Cloud over Clarence. Marc Brown. Ill. by the author. Unicorn/Dutton.
32 pp. (1980).

Cloudy with a Chance of Meatballs. Judi Barrett. Ill. by Ron Barrett.
Atheneum. 32 pp. (1979).

Come Away from the Water, Shirley. John Burningham. Ill. by the author.
Crowell. 22 pp. (1978).

The Compost Heap. Harlow Rockwell. Ill. by the author. Doubleday. 24 pp.
(1974).

Cora Copycat. Helen Lester. Ill. by the author. Dutton. 32 pp. (1980).

Cowardly Clyde. Bill Peet. Ill. by the author. Houghton. 40 pp. (1980).

Crackle Gluck and the Sleeping Toad. Dick Gackenbach. Ill. by the author.
Houghton/Clarion. 32 pp. (1980).

Cranberry Christmas. Wende and Harry Devlin. Ill. by Harry Devlin. Parents.
29 pp. (1977).

Crocus. Roger Duvoisin. Ill. by the author. Knopf. 29 pp. (1978).

Cross-Country Cat. Mary Calhoun. Ill. by Erick Ingraham. Morrow. 42 pp.
(1980).

Crystal Is the New Girl. Shirley Gordon. Ill. by Edward Frascino. Harper.
32 pp. (1977).

Cunningham's Rooster. Barbara Brenner. Ill. by Anne Rockwell. Parents.
28 pp. (1975). O/P

Daddy. Jeannette Caines. Ill. by Ronald Himler. Harper. 32 pp. (1978).

Dawn. Uri Shulevitz. Ill. by the author. Farrar. 32 pp. (1974).

The Day I Was Born. Marjorie Weinman Sharmat & Mitchell Sharmat. Ill. by
Diane Dawson. Dutton. 32 pp. (1981).

The Day Jimmy's Boa Ate the Wash. Trinka Hakes Noble. Ill. by Steven
Kellogg. Dial. 32 pp. (1981).

Deep in the Forest. Brinton Turkle. Dutton. 32 pp. (1977).

The Desert Is Theirs. Byrd Baylor. Ill. by Peter Parnall. Scribner. 32 pp. (1975).
P, Atheneum.

Dig, Drill, Dump, Fill. Tana Hoban. Photos by the author. Greenwillow. 32 pp.
(1975).

Dinner at Alberta's. Russell Hoban. Ill. by James Marshall. Crowell. 40 pp.
(1975). P, Dell.

Dinosaur's Housewarming Party. Norma Klein. Ill. by James Marshall.
Crown. 39 pp. (1974).

The Discontented Mother. Ben Shecter. Ill. by the author. Harcourt. 32 pp.
(1981).

The Dog Who Insisted He Wasn't. Marilyn Singer. Ill. by Kelly Oechsli. Dutton.
32 pp. (1977). O/P

Don't Forget the Bacon! Pat Hutchins. Ill. by the author. Greenwillow. 32 pp.
(1977). P, Puffin.

Dreams. Ezra Jack Keats. Ill. by the author. Macmillan. 33 pp. (1974). P,
Macmillan.

The Easter Egg Artists. Adrienne Adams. Ill. by the author. Scribner. 32 pp.
(1977). P, Atheneum.

Ed Emberley's ABC. Ed Emberley. Ill. by the author. Little, Brown. 62 pp.
(1979).

Ed Emberley's Drawing Book of Faces. Ed Emberley. Ill. by the author. Little,
Brown. 32 pp. (1975).

An Elephant in My Bed. Suzanne Klein. Ill. by Sharleen Pederson. Follett. 31 pp. (1974). O/P.

The Elephant's Ball. Evelyne Johnson. Ill. by Tien. McGraw. 40 pp. (1978).

Eric Carle's Storybook: Seven Tales by the Brothers Grimm. Eric Carle. Ill. by the author. Watts. 94 pp. (1977). O/P.

Everett Anderson's 1-2-3. Lucille Clifton. Ill. by Ann Grifalconi. Holt. 27 pp. (1978).

Everett Anderson's Year. Lucille Clifton. Ill. by Ann Grifalconi. Holt. 31 pp. (1974).

The Everyday Train. Amy Ehrlich. Ill. by Martha Alexander. Dial. 27 pp. (1978).

The Family Minus. Fernando Krahn. Ill. by the author. Parents. 32 pp. (1978). O/P.

Farmer Palmer's Wagon Ride. William Steig. Ill. by the author. Farrar. 32 pp. (1974). P, Puffin.

The Field of Buttercups. Alice Boden. Ill. by the author. Walck. 32 pp. (1975). O/P.

First Grade Takes a Test. Miriam Cohen. Ill. by Lillian Hoban. Greenwillow. 32 pp. (1981).

A Flea Story: I Want to Stay Here! I Want to Go There! Leo Lionni. Ill. by the author. Pantheon. 32 pp. (1978).

Fog in the Meadow. Joanne Ryder. Ill. by Gail Owens. Harper. 32 pp. (1980).

The Foundling. Carol Carrick. Ill. by Donald Carrick. Clarion/Houghton. 29 pp. (1978).

Fox Eyes. Margaret Wise Brown. Ill. by Garth Williams. Pantheon. 32 pp. (1978).

Frederick's Alligator. Esther Allen Peterson. Ill. by Susanna Natti. Crown. 36 pp. (1980). P, Scholastic.

Friends Are Like That! Selected by The Child Study Children's Book Committee at Bank Street. Ill. by Leigh Grant. Crowell. 114 pp. (1980).

George and Martha One Fine Day. James Marshall. Ill. by the author. Houghton. 46 pp. (1979).

George the Babysitter. Shirley Hughes. Ill. by the author. Prentice. 32 pp. (1979).

Georgie's Christmas Carol. Robert Bright. Ill. by the author. Doubleday. 48 pp. (1975).

Gertie and Gus. Lisl Weil. Ill. by the author. Parents'. 29 pp. (1978). O/P.

Giants, Indeed! Virginia Kahl. Ill. by the author. Scribner. 32 pp. (1974).

The Girl on the Yellow Giraffe. Ronald Himler. Ill. by the author. Harper. 32 pp. (1977). O/P.

The Great Big Elephant and the Very Small Elephant. Barbara Seuling. Ill. by the author. Crown. 36 pp. (1978). P, Scholastic.

The Great Valentine's Day Balloon Race. Adrienne Adams. Ill. by the author. Scribner. 32 pp. (1981).

Gregory Griggs and Other Nursery Rhyme People. Arnold Lobel. Ill. by the author. Greenwillow. 47 pp. (1979).

Gregory, the Terrible Eater. Mitchell Sharmat. Ill. by Jose Aruego and Ariane Dewey. Four Winds. 32 pp. (1981).

The Grouchy Ladybug. Eric Carle. Ill. by the author. Crowell. 48 pp. (1978).

Grumley the Grouch. Marjorie Weinman Sharmat. Ill. by Kay Chorao. Holiday. 32 pp. (1981).

Hamilton. Robert Newton Park. Ill. by Laura Lydecker. Little, Brown. 32 pp. (1976).

Hang On, Hester!. Wende Davlin and Harry Devlin. Ill. by Harry Devlin. Lothrop. 48 pp. (1981).

Hansel and Gretel. The Brothers Grimm. Ill. by Susan Jeffers. Dial. 32 pp. (1981).

Harriet Goes to the Circus. Betsy Maestro. Ill. by Giulio Maestro. Crown. 29 pp. (1978).

Harry and the Terrible Whatzit. Dick Gackenbach. Ill. by the author. Clarion/ Houghton. 32 pp. (1978). P, Scholastic.

Hector and Christina. Louise Fatio. Ill. by Roger Duvoisin. McGraw. 32 pp. (1978).

Herman the Helper. Robert Kraus. Ill. by Jose Aruego and Ariane Dewey. Windmill. 32 pp. (1974). P, Windmill.

Hester in the Wild. Sandra Boynton. Ill. by the author. Harper. 32 pp. (1980). P, Harper.

Hiccup. Mercer Mayer. Ill. by the author. Dial. 29 pp. (1977). P, Dial.

The Hiding Game. Ben Shecter. Ill. by the author. Parents. 27 pp. (1978).

Hippos Go Berserk. Sandra Boynton. Ill. by the author. Little, Brown. 32 pp. (1980). P, Little, Brown.

His Mother's Dog. Liesel Skorpen. Ill. by M.E. Mullin. Harper. 46 pp. (1979).

Hooray for Pig. Carla Stevens. Ill. by Rainey Bennett. Seabury. 48 pp. (1974).

How the Rooster Saved the Day. Arnold Lobel. Ill. by Anita Lobel. Green-willow. 28 pp. (1978). P, Puffin.

How to Dig a Hole to the Other Side of the World. Faith McNulty. Ill. by Marc Simont. Harper. 32 pp. (1980).

Humbug Rabbit. Lorna Balian. Ill. by the author. Abingdon. 32 pp. (1974).

Hush Up! Jim Aylesworth. Ill. by Glen Rounds. Holt. 32 pp. (1981).

I Am Not a Pest. Marjorie Weinman Sharmat and Mitchell Sharmat. Ill. by Diane Dawson. Dutton. 32 pp. (1980).

I Know an Old Lady Who Swallowed a Fly. Retold by Nadine Bernard West-cott. Ill. by the author. Atlantic-Little, Brown. 40 pp. (1981). P, Atlantic-Little, Brown.

I Like the Library. Anne Rockwell. Ill. by the author. Dutton. 28 pp. (1978).

I Sure Am Glad to See You Blackboard Bear. Martha Alexander. Ill. by the author. Dial. 32 pp. (1977). P, Dial.

I Want to Be Big. Genie Iverson. Ill. by David McPhail. Unicorn/Dutton. 32 pp. (1980).

If I Could Be My Grandmother. Steven Kroll. Ill. by Lady McCrady. Pantheon. 30 pp. (1978).

If I Had My Way. Norma Klein. Ill. by Ray Cruz. Pantheon. 33 pp. (1974).

If I Were a Toad. Diane Paterson. Ill. by the author. Dial. 29 pp. (1978).

If You Say So, Claude. Joan Lowery Nixon. Ill. by Lorinda Bryan Cauley. Warne. 48 pp. (1981).

I'm Not Oscar's Friend Anymore. Marjorie Weinman Sharmat. Ill. by Tony DeLuna. Dutton. 32 pp. (1975).

It's Not Fair! Robyn Supraner. Ill. by Randall Enos. Warne. 32 pp. (1977).

It's Time to Go to Bed. Joyce Segal. Ill. by Robin Eaton. Doubleday. 32 pp. (1980).

Ivan, Divan, and Zariman. Marta Koci. Ill. by the author. Parents. 28 pp. (1978). O/P.

Jack-O'-Lantern. Edna Barth. Ill. by Paul Galdone. Clarion/Houghton. 48 pp. (1974).

Jamie's Tiger. Jan Wahl. Ill. by Tomie de Paola. Harcourt. 48 pp. (1979).

Jenny Learns a Lesson. Gyo Fujikawa. Ill. by the author. Grossett. 32 pp. (1981).

Jeremy Isn't Hungry. Barbara Williams. Ill. by Martha Alexander. Dutton. 30 pp. (1979).

Jethro's Difficult Dinosaur. Arnold Sundgaard. Ill. by Stan Mack. Pantheon. 26 pp. (1978).

Jill the Pill. Julie Castiglia. Ill. by Steven Kellogg. McElderry/Atheneum. 32 pp. (1980).

John Brown, Rose and the Midnight Cat. Jenny Wagner. Ill. by Ron Brooks. Bradbury. 32 pp. (1979). P, Puffin.

Keep Out. Noela Young. Ill. by the author. Philomel. 32 pp. (1978).

The King at the Door. Brock Cole. Ill. by the author. Doubleday. 32 pp. (1980).

King Rollo and the Bread. King Rollo and the Birthday. King Rollo and the New Shoes (set of three). David McKee. Ill. by the author. Atlantic-Little, Brown. 32 pp. each. (1981).

The King's Cat is Coming. Stan Mack. Ill. by the author. Pantheon. 28 pp. (1977).

The King's Flower. Mitsumasa Anno. Ill. by the author. Philomel. 32 pp. (1980).

Kittens for Nothing. Robert Kraus. Ill. by Diane Paterson. Windmill. 27 pp. (1977).

Kittymouse. Sumiko. Ill. by the author. Harcourt. 30 pp. (1980).

The Lady Who Saw the Good Side of Everything. Pat Decker Tapio. Ill. by Paul Galdone. Clarion/Houghton. 32 pp. (1975).

Laura's Story. Beatrice Schenk de Regniers. Ill. by Jack Kent. Atheneum. 32 pp. (1980).

Little Koala. Suzanne Noguere and Tony Chen. Ill. by Tony Chen. Holt. 32 pp. (1980).

Little Love Story. Fernando Krahn. Lippincott. 24 pp. (1977).

Little One Inch. Barbara Brenner. Ill. by Fred Brenner. Coward. 28 pp. (1978).

Little Rabbit's Loose Tooth. Lucy Bate. Ill. by Diane DeGroat. Crown. 28 pp. (1975). P, Scholastic.

The Little Worm Book. Janet Ahlberg and Allan Ahlberg. Ill. by the authors. Viking. 32 pp. (1981).

Louie. Ezra Jack Keats. Ill. by the author. Greenwillow. 32 pp. (1975). P, Scholastic.

Love from Uncle Clyde. Nancy Winslow Parker. Ill. by the author. Dial. 32 pp. (1978).

Lyle Finds His Mother. Bernard Waber. Ill. by the author. Houghton. 48 pp. (1974). P, Houghton.

Maggie and the Goodbye Gift. Sue Milord. Ill. by Jerry Milord. Lothrop. 40 pp. (1980).

The Maggie B. Irene Haas. Ill. by the author. Atheneum/McElderry. 28 pp. (1975).

The Magic Meatballs. Alan Yaffe. Ill. by Karen Born Andersen. Dial. 38 pp. (1980).

The Magic Porridge Pot. Paul Galdone. Ill. by the author. Clarion/Houghton. 30 pp. (1977).

Marie Louise and Christophe. Natalie Savage Carlson. Ill. by Jose Aruego and Ariane Dewey. Scribner. 40 pp. (1974).

Martha's Mad Day. Miranda Hapgood. Ill. by Emily McCully. Crown. 29 pp. (1978). O/P.

Mary Alice Operator Number 9. Jeffrey Allen. Ill. by James Marshall. Little, Brown. 26 pp. (1975). P, Puffin.

Maude and Claude Go Aboard. Susan Meddaugh. Ill. by the author. Houghton. 32 pp. (1981).

Max. Rachel Isadora. Ill. by the author. Macmillan. 32 pp. (1977).

Mean Maxine. Barbara Bottner. Ill. by the author. Pantheon. 32 pp. (1981).

Messy. Barbara Bottner. Ill. by the author. Delacorte. 32 pp. (1980).

Michael. Liesel Moak Skorpen. Ill. by Joan Sardin. Harper. 41 pp. (1975).

Miss Kiss and the Nasty Beast. Lady McCrady. Ill. by the author. Holiday. 32 pp. (1980).

Molly and the Slow Teeth. Pat Ross. Ill. by Jerry Milord. Lothrop. 48 pp. (1981).

Monster Mary Mischief Maker. Kazuko Taniguchi. Ill. by the author. McGraw. 37 pp. (1977).

The Monster Riddle Book. Jane Sarnoff and Reynold Ruffins. Ill. by the authors. Scribner. 30 pp. (1975).

Mooch the Messy Meets Prudence the Neat. Marjorie Weinman Sharmat. Ill. by Ben Shecter. Coward. 64 pp. (1980).

Morris and Boris. Bernard Wiseman. Ill. by the author. Dodd. 64 pp. (1974).

The Most Amazing Hide-and-Seek Alphabet Book. Robert Crowther. Viking. 12 pp. (1978).

A Mouse Called Junction. Julia Cunningham. Ill. by Michael Hague. Pantheon. 32 pp. (1981).

Mouse Six and the Happy Birthday. Miska Miles. Ill. by Leslie Morrill. Unicorn/Dutton. 32 pp. (1979).

Mousekin's Close Call. Edna Miller. Ill. by the author. Prentice. 32 pp. (1979). P, Prentice.

Mr. and Mrs. Button's Wonderful Watchdogs. Janice. Ill. by Roger Duvoisin. Lothrop. 29 pp. (1979).

Mr. and Mrs. Pig's Evening Out. Mary Rayner. Ill. by the author. Atheneum. 32 pp. (1977). P, Atheneum.

Mr. Goat's Bad Good Idea. Marileta Robinson. Ill. by Arthur Getz. Crowell. 46 pp. (1980).

Mr. Grumpy's Motor Car. John Burningham. Ill. by the author. Crowell. 30 pp. (1977). P, Puffin.

Mrs. Gaddy and the Ghost. Wilson Gage. Ill. by Marilyn Hafner. Greenwillow. 60 pp. (1980).

Mrs. Peloki's Snake. Joanne Oppenheim. Ill. by Joyce Audy dos Santos. Dodd. 32 pp. (1981).

Ms. Klondike. Jessica Ross. Ill. by the author. Viking. 28 pp. (1978). O/P.

Mushroom in the Rain. Mirra Ginsburg. Ill. by Jose Aruego and Ariane Dewey. Macmillan. 32 pp. (1974). P, Macmillan.

My Brother Never Feeds the Cat. Reynold Ruffins. Ill. by the author. Scribner. 32 pp. (1980).

My Friend, Jasper Jones. Rosamond Dauer. Ill. by Jerry Joyner. Parents. 27 pp. (1978). O/P.

My Mothers Didn't Kiss Me Good-Night. Charlotte Herman. Ill. by Bruce Degen. Dutton. 32 pp. (1981).

My Very Own Octopus. Bernard Most. Ill. by the author. Harcourt. 32 pp. (1981).

The Mysterious Tadpole. Steven Kellogg. Ill. by the author. Dial. 20 pp. (1978). P, Dial.

The Mystery of the Giant Footprints. Fernando Krahn. Dutton. 32 pp. (1978).

The Mystery of the Missing Red Mitten. Steven Kellogg. Ill. by the author. Dial. 32 pp. (1974). P, Dial.

Nate the Great and the Sticky Case. Marjorie Weinman Sharmat. Ill. by Marc Simont. Coward. 48 pp. (1979). P, Dell.

The New Girl at School. Judy Delton. Ill. by Lillian Hoban. Dutton. 32 pp. (1980).

Next Year I'll Be Special. Patricia Reilly Giff. Ill. by Marilyn Hafner. Dutton. 32 pp. (1981).

No Dogs Allowed, Jonathan! Mary Blount Christian. Ill. by Don Madden. Addison. 32 pp. (1975).

Noah's Ark. Peter Spier. Doubleday. 44 pp. (1978). P, Doubleday.
Nobody Stole the Pie. Sonia Levitin. Ill. by Fernando Krahn. Harcourt. 32 pp. (1981). P, Harcourt.
Old Mother Hubbard and Her Dog. Sarah C. Martin. Ill. by Ib Spang Olsen. Coward. 32 pp. (1977). O/P.
Oliver and Alison's Week. Jane Breskin Zalben. Ill. by Emily Arnold McCully. Farrar. 40 pp. (1981).
Oliver Button is a Sissy. Tomie de Paola. Ill. by the author. Harcourt. 48 pp. (1980). P, Harcourt.
One Big Wish. Jay Williams. Ill. by John O'Brien. Macmillan. 32 pp. (1981).
One Dragon to Another. Ned Delaney. Ill. by the author. Houghton. 48 pp. (1977).
One-Eyed Jake. Pat Hutchins. Ill. by the author. Greenwillow. 32 pp. (1980).
One, Two, Three—Ah-Choo! Marjorie N. Allen. Ill. by Dick Gackenbach. Coward. 64 pp. (1981).
Otter in the Cove. Miska Miles. Ill. by John Schoenherr. Atlantic-Little, Brown. 48 pp. (1974).
Owliver. Robert Kraus. Ill. by Jose Aruego and Ariane Dewey. Windmill. 32 pp. (1974). P, Windmill.
Owl's New Cards. Kathryn Ernst. Ill. by Diane de Groat. Crown. 30 pp. (1978).
Paddy Pork's Holiday. John S. Goodall. Atheneum/McElderry. 59 pp. (1977).
The Pancake. Anita Lobel. Ill. by the author. Greenwillow. 48 pp. (1979).
Pancakes for Breakfast. Tomie de Paola. Ill by the author. Harcourt. 32 pp. (1979). P, Harcourt.
Paper Party. Don Freeman. Ill. by the author. Viking. 40 pp. (1974). P, Puffin.
Paul's Christmas Birthday. Carol Carrick. Ill. by Donald Carrick. Greenwillow. 32 pp. (1979).
Peace at Last. Jill Murphy. Ill. by the author. Dial. 32 pp. (1981).
Pettifur. Jay Williams. Ill. by Hilary Knight. Four Winds. 35 pp. (1978). O/P.
Pig Pig Grows Up. David McPhail. Ill. by the author. Dutton/Unicorn. 24 pp. (1981).
A Pocket for Corduroy. Don Freeman. Ill. by the author. Viking. 26 pp. (1979). P, Puffin.
Poor Goose: A French Folktale. Anne Rockwell. Ill. by the author. Crowell. 34 pp. (1977).
Portly McSwine. James Marshall. Ill. by the author. Houghton. 40 pp. (1980).
Potato Pancakes All Around: A Hanukkah Tale. Marilyn Hirsh. Ill. by the author. Bonim. 32 pp. (1979).
The Quiet House. Otto Coontz. Ill. by the author. Little, Brown. 39 pp. (1979).
Rabbit Finds a Way. Judy Delton. Ill. by Joe Lasker. Crown. 32 pp. (1975).
Rainy Rainy Saturday. Jack Prelutsky. Ill. by Marilyn Hafner. Greenwillow. 48 pp. (1981).
Rebecca Hatpin. Robert Kraus. Ill. by Robert Byrd. Windmill/Dutton. 32 pp. (1974). O/P.
Robot-Bot-Bot. Fernando Krahn. Ill. by the author. Dutton. 32 pp. (1980).
Rodney Peppe's Puzzle Book. Rodney Peppe. Viking. 24 pp. (1978). O/P.
Rotten Ralph. Jack Gantos. Ill. by Nicole Rubel. Houghton. 48 pp. (1977). P, Houghton.
Ruby. Amy Aitken. Ill. by the author. Bradbury. 32 pp. (1980).
Rum Pum Pum. Retold by Maggie Duff. Ill. by Jose Aruego and Ariane Dewey. Macmillan. 32 pp. (1979).
The Runaway Pancake. P. Chr. Asbjornsen and Jorgen Moe. Trans. from the Danish by Joan Tate. Ill. by Svend Otto S. Larousse. 32 pp. (1981).
Sam Who Never Forgets. Eve Rice. Ill. by the author. Greenwillow. 30 pp. (1978). P, Puffin.

Sara and the Door. Virginia Allen Jensen. Ill. by Ann Strugnell. Addison. 26 pp. (1978).

The Seal and the Slick. Don Freeman. Ill. by the author. Viking. 32 pp. (1974).

The Seeing Stick. Jane Yolen. Ill. by Remy Charlip and Demetra Maraslis. Crowell. 26 pp. (1978).

Send Wendell. Genevieve Gray. Ill. by Symeon Shimin. McGraw. 32 pp. (1974). O/P.

729 Curious Creatures. Helen Oxenbury. Ill. by the author. Harper. 18 pp. (1981).

Seven Little Monsters. Maurice Sendak. Harper. 16 pp. (1978). P, Harper.

She Come Bringing Me That Little Baby Girl. Eloise Greenfield. Ill. by John Steptoe. Lippincott. 32 pp. (1974).

Six Little Ducks. Chris Conover. Crowell. 27 pp. (1977).

Small Rabbit. Miska Miles. Ill. by Jim Arnosky. Atlantic-Little, Brown. 31 pp. (1978).

The Snake: A Very Long Story. Bernard Waber. Ill. by the author. Houghton. 48 pp. (1979).

The Snowman. Raymond Briggs. Ill. by the author. Random. 32 pp. (1979).

Socks for Supper. Jack Kent. Ill. by the author. Parents. 32 pp. (1979).

Spots Are Special. Kathryn Osebald Galbraith. Ill. by Diane Dawson. Atheneum/McElderry. 27 pp. (1977).

Squeeze a Sneeze. Bill Morrison. Ill. by the author. Houghton. 30 pp. (1978).

The Stonecutter. Gerald McDermott. Ill. by the author. Viking. 28 pp. (1975). P, Puffin.

The Strongest One of All. Mirra Ginsburg. Ill. by Jose Aruego and Ariane Dewey. Greenwillow. 32 pp. (1978).

The Stupids Have a Ball. Harry Allard and James Marshall. Ill. by James Marshall. Houghton. 31 pp. (1979).

The Substitute. Ann Lawler. Ill. by Nancy Winslow Parker. Parents. 32 pp. (1978). O/P.

The Summer Night. Charlotte Zolotow. Ill. by Ben Shecter. Harper. 32 pp. (1974).

Summer on Cleo's Island. Natalie G. Sylvester. Ill. by the author. Farrar. 37 pp. (1978).

The Sweet Touch. Lorna Balian. Ill. by the author. Abingdon. 37 pp. (1977).

The Tailypo. Joanna Galdone. Ill. by Paul Galdone. Clarion/Houghton. 30 pp. (1978).

Taking Care of Melvin. Marjorie Weinman Sharmat. Ill. by Victoria Chess. Holiday. 32 pp. (1981).

The Tale of Meshka the Kvetch. Carol Chapman. Ill. by Arnold Lobel. Dutton. 32 pp. (1981).

The Tale of Thomas Mead. Pat Hutchins. Ill. by the author. Greenwillow. 32 pp. (1981).

The Terrible Troll-Bird. Ingri and Edgar Parin d'Aulair. Ill. by the authors. Doubleday. 45 pp. (1977).

That Terrible Halloween Night. James Stevenson. Ill. by the author. Greenwillow. 32 pp. (1981).

There's an Elephant in the Garbage. Douglas F. Davis. Ill. by Steven Kellogg. Dutton. 32 pp. (1980).

Thorn Rose or The Sleeping Beauty. The Brothers Grimm. Ill. by Errol Le Cain. Bradbury. 32 pp. (1978). P, Puffin.

Those Terrible Toy-Breakers. David McPhail. Ill. by the author. Parents. 48 pp. (1981).

Three Ducks Went Wandering. Ron Roy. Ill. by Paul Galdone. Clarion/Houghton. 32 pp. (1980). P, Scholastic.

Three Wishes. Lucille Clifton. Ill. by Stephanie Douglas. Viking. 32 pp. (1977). O/P.

The Tiger-Skin Rug. Gerald Rose. Ill. by the author. Prentice. 32 pp. (1980).

Today Was a Terrible Day. Patricia Reilly Giff. Ill. by Susanna Natti. Viking. 32 pp. (1981).

The Tortoise and the Tree. Janina Domanska. Ill. by the author. Greenwillow. 32 pp. (1979).

A Treeful of Pigs. Arnold Lobel. Ill. by Anita Lobel. Greenwillow. 32 pp. (1980).

The Trip. Ezra Jack Keats. Ill. by the author. Greenwillow. 32 pp. (1979). P, Scholastic.

Troll Country. Edward Marshall. Ill. by James Marshall. Dial. 56 pp. (1981). P, Dial.

The Tutti-Frutti Case. Harry Allard. Ill. by James Marshall. Prentice. 32 pp. (1975).

Two Good Friends. Judy Delton. Ill. by Giulio Maestro. Crown. 32 pp. (1974).

Two Greedy Bears. Mirra Ginsburg. Ill. by Jose Aruego and Ariane Dewey. Macmillan. 32 pp. (1977).

Tyler Toad and the Thunder. Robert L. Crowe. Ill. by Kay Chorao. Dutton. 32 pp. (1981).

The Tyrannosaurus Game. Steven Kroll. Ill. by Tomie de Paola. Holiday. 40 pp. (1977).

The Unexpected Grandchildren. Jane Flory. Ill. by Carolyn Croll. Houghton. 32 pp. (1978).

A Very Young Circus Flyer. Jill Krementz. Photographs by the author. Knopf. 110 pp. (1980).

The Visit. Diane Wolkstein. Ill. by Lois Ehlert. Knopf. 29 pp. (1978).

Watch Out for Chicken Feet in Your Soup. Tomie de Paola. Ill. by the author. Prentice. 32 pp. (1974). .

We Hide, You Seek. Jose Aruego and Ariane Dewey. Ill. by the authors. Greenwillow. 32 pp. (1980).

Welcome is a Wonderful Word. Gyo Gujikawa. Ill. by the author. Grosset. 32 pp. (1981).

The Werewolf Family. Jack Gantos. Ill. by Nicole Rubel. Houghton. 32 pp. (1981).

What Should a Hippo Wear? Jane Sutton. Ill. by Lynn Munsinger. Houghton. 32 pp. (1980).

What the Moon Saw. Brian Wildsmith. Ill. by the author. Oxford. 32 pp. (1979).

What's Happening to Daisy? Sandy Rabinowitz. Harper. 32 pp. (1978).

When the Wind Stops. Charlotte Zolotow. Ill. by Howard Knotts. Harper. 32 pp. (1975).

Where Can an Elephant Hide? David McPhail. Ill. by the author. Doubleday. 30 pp. (1980).

Where Did My Mother Go? Edna Mitchell Preston. Ill. by Chris Conover. Four Winds. 29 pp. (1979).

Where Does the Sun Go at Night? Mirra Ginsburg. Ill. by Jose Aruego and Ariane Dewey. Greenwillow. 32 pp. (1981).

Where's Mark? Jacquie Hann. Ill. by the author. Four Winds. 34 pp. (1978).

Where's My Hippopotamus? Mark Alan Stamaty. Ill. by the author. Dial. 30 pp. (1978). P, Dial.

Which is the Witch? W.K. Jasner. Ill. by Victoria Chess. Pantheon. 48 pp. (1980).

Why Mosquitoes Buzz in People's Ears. Verna Aardema. Ill. by Leo Dillon and Diane Dillon. Dial. 32 pp. (1975). P, Dial.

Wild Robin. Susan Jeffers. Ill. by the author. Dutton. 40 pp. (1977).

Will It Be Okay? Crescent Dragonwagon. Ill. by Ben Shecter. Harper. 32 pp. (1978).

Willaby. Rachel Isadora. Ill. by the author. Macmillan. 30 pp. (1978).

The Wobbly Tooth. Nancy Evans Cooney. Ill. by Marilin Hafner. Putnam. 32 pp. (1979). P, Putnam.

A Worm for Dinner. Ned Delaney. Ill. by the author. Houghton. 32 pp. (1978).

The Worst Person in the World. James Stevenson. Ill. by the author. Greenwillow. 32 pp. (1979). P, Puffin.

The Wounded Wolf. Jean Craighead George. Ill. by John Schoenherr. Harper. 32 pp. (1979).

Wriggles, The Little Wishing Pig. Pauline Watson. Ill. by Paul Galdone. Clarion/Houghton. 32 pp. (1979).

The Wuggie Norple Story. Daniel M. Pinkwater. Ill. by Tomie de Paola. Four Winds. 40 pp. (1981).

You're the Scaredy-Cat. Mercer Mayer. Ill. by the author. Parents. 40 pp. (1974).

Zoo City. Stephen Lewis. Photographs by the author. Greenwillow. 32 pp. (1977).

Middle Grades

Abracadabra! Barbara Seuling. Ill. by the author. Messner. 96 pp. (1975). O/P.

The Accident. Carol Carrick. Ill. by Donald Carrick. Clarion/Houghton. 32 pp. (1977). P, Clarion/Houghton.

The Against Taffy Sinclair Club. Betsy Haynes. Lodestar/Dutton. 125 pp. (1977). P, Bantam.

Aldo Applesauce. Johanna Hurwitz. Ill. by John Wallner. Morrow. 128 pp. (1980).

All the Children Were Sent Away. Sheila Garrigue. Bradbury. 171 pp. (1977).

All the Money in the World. Bill Brittain. Ill. by Charles Robinson. Harper. 160 pp. (1980).

All Upon a Sidewalk. Jean Craighead George. Ill. by Don Bolognese. Dutton. 48 pp. (1974).

Anastasia Krupnik. Lois Lowry. Houghton. 160 pp. (1980). P, Bantam.

Animals and Their Ears. Olive L. Earle and Michael Kantor. Ill. by the author. Morrow. 64 pp. (1974).

Bad Luck Tony. Dennis Fradin. Ill. by Joanne Scribner. Prentice. 40 pp. (1979).

Beat the Turtle Drum. Constance C. Greene. Ill. by Donna Diamond. Viking. 119 pp. (1977). P, Dell.

Becky and the Bear. Dorothy van Woerkom. Ill. by Margot Tomes. Putnam. 34 pp. (1975).

The Best Burglar Alarm. Brenda Seabrooke. Ill. by Loretta Lustig. Morrow. 30 pp. (1979).

Big Anthony and the Magic Ring. Tomie de Paola. Ill. by the author. Harcourt. 32 pp. (1980). P, Harcourt.

The Big Cats. Herbert S. Zim. Ill. by Dot Barlowe. Morrow. 64 pp. (1977).

The Big Orange Splot. Daniel Manus Pinkwater. Ill. by the author. Hastings. 32 pp. (1978). P, Scholastic.

The Blue Lobster. Carol Carrick. Ill. by Donald Carrick. Dial. 26 pp. (1975).

Bunnicula. Deborah Howe and James Howe. Ill. by Alan Daniel. Atheneum. 112 pp. (1980). P, Avon.

Bus Station Mystery. Gertrude Chandler Warner. Ill. by David Cunningham. Albert Whitman. 125 pp. (1974).

A Calf is Born. Joanna Cole. Photographs by Jerome Wexler. Morrow. 48 pp. (1975).

Captain Toad and the Motorbike. David McPhail. Ill. by the author. McElderry/Atheneum. 29 pp. (1979).

The Case of the Nervous Newsboy. E.W. Hildick. Ill. by Lisl Weil. Macmillan. 106 pp. (1977). P, Pocket.

The Case of the Phantom Frog. E.W. Hildick. Ill. by Lisl Weil. Macmillan. 122 pp. (1980). P, Pocket.

The Case of the Silver Skull. Scott Corbett. Ill. by Paul Frame. Atlantic-Little, Brown. 123 pp. (1974).

The Case of the Vanishing Boy. Alexander Key. Pocket (paperback). 212 pp. (1980).

Charles Bear and the Mystery of the Forest. Douglas Adamson. Ill. by the author. Houghton. 87 pp. (1978).

Chester. Mary Francis Shura. Ill. by Susan Swan. Dodd. 96 pp. (1981).

A Chocolate Moose for Dinner. Fred Gwynne. Ill. by the author. Windmill. 64 pp. (1977).

The Church Mice Spread Their Wings. Graham Oakley. Atheneum. 32 pp. (1977).

Cinderella. Retold by Paul Galdone. Ill. by the author. McGraw. 40 pp. (1979).

The Clown of God. Tomie de Paola. Ill. by the author. Harcourt. 47 pp. (1979). P, Harcourt.

Clyde Monster. Robert L. Crowe. Ill. by Kay Chorao. Dutton. 27 pp. (1977).

Cookie Becker Casts a Spell. Lee Glazer. Ill. by Margot Apple. Little, Brown. 48 pp. (1981).

Crazy in Love. Richard Kennedy. Ill. by Marcia Sewall. Dutton/Unicorn. 64 pp. (1981).

Cross Your Fingers, Spit in Your Hat: Superstitions and Other Beliefs. Collected by Alvin Schwartz. Ill. by Glen Rounds. Lippincott. 159 pp. (1974).

Danbury's Burning! The Story of Sybil Ludington's Ride. Anne Grant. Ill. by Pat Howell. Walck. 47 pp. (1977). O/P.

Danny. Roald Dahl. Knopf. 224 pp. (1975).

Danny Dunn, Invisible Boy. Jay Williams and Ray Abrashkin. Ill. by Paul Sagsoorian. McGraw. 159 pp. (1974). P, Pocket.

The Difference of Ari Stein. Charlotte Herman. Ill. by Ben Shecter. Harper. 150 pp. (1977).

Do You Love Me? Dick Gackenbach. Ill. by the author. Clarion/Houghton. 48 pp. (1975). P, Dell.

Don't Feel Sorry for Paul. Bernard Wolf. Photographs by the author. Lippincott. 96 pp. (1974).

The Door. Jacklyn O'Hanlon. Dial. 88 pp. (1979).

Dracula. Bram Stoker. Adapted by Alice Schick and Joel Schick. Ill. by the adapters. Delacorte. 48 pp. (1981). P, Delacorte.

Dracula's Cat. Jan Wahl. Ill. by Kay Chorao. Prentice. 28 pp. (1979).

The Ears of Louis. Constance Greene. Ill. by Nola Langner. Viking. 89 pp. (1974).

Encyclopedia Brown Lends a Hand. Donald J. Sobol. Ill. by Leonard Shortall. Lodestar/Dutton. 95 pp. (1974).

Escape King. John Ernst. Ill. by Ray Abel. Prentice. 28 pp. (1975). P, Prentice.

Everyone Knows What a Dragon Looks Like. Jay Williams. Ill. by Mercer Mayer. Four Winds. 28 pp. (1977). P, Scholastic.

Fanny's Sister. Penelope Lively. Ill. by Anita Lobel. Dutton. 64 pp. (1981).

Football Players Do Amazing Things. Mel Cebulash. Ill. with photographs. Random. 72 pp. (1975).

Four Scary Stories. Tony Johnston. Ill. by Tomie de Paola. Putnam. 30 pp. (1979). P, Putnam.

Free to Be...You and Me. Marlo Thomas. McGraw. 138 pp. (1974).
Front Court Hex. Matt Christopher. Ill. by Byron Goto. Little, Brown. 136 pp. (1974).
The Frog Band and Durrington Dormouse. Jim Smith. Ill. by the author. Little, Brown. 32 pp. (1979).
The Frog Band and the Onion Seller. Jim Smith. Ill. by the author. Little, Brown. 32 pp. (1978). P, Little, Brown.
Getting Along in Your Family. Phyllis Reynolds Naylor. Ill. by Rick Cooley. Abingdon. 107 pp. (1977).
The Ghost on Saturday Night. Sid Fleischman. Ill. by Eric Von Schmidt. Atlantic-Little, Brown. 63 pp. (1974).
Ghosts. Seymour Simon. Ill. by Stephen Gammell. Lippincott. 76 pp. (1977). P, Lippincott.
The Gift-Giver. Joyce Hansen. Clarion/Houghton. 128 pp. (1981).
The Girl Who Loved Wild Horses. Paul Gobel. Ill. by the author. Bradbury. 32 pp. (1979).
Good-Bye, Chicken Little. Betsy Byars. Harper. 112 pp. (1980).
Good Work, Amelia Bedelia. Peggy Parish. Ill. by Lynn Sweat. Greenwillow. 56 pp. (1977). P, Avon.
The Goof That Won the Pennant. Jonah Kalb. Ill. by Sandy Kassin. Houghton. 103 pp. (1977).
Grandpa's Ghost Stories. James Flora. Ill. by the author. McElderry/Atheneum. 32 pp. (1979). P, Atheneum.
The Great Brain Does It Again. John D. Fitzgerald. Ill. by Mercer Mayer. Dial. 127 pp. (1975). P, Dell.
The Great Custard Pie Panic. Scott Corbett. Ill. by Joe Mathieu. Atlantic-Little, Brown. 48 pp. (1974). P, Scholastic.
The Great Pete Penney. Jean Bashor Tolle. McElderry/Atheneum. 112 pp. (1980).
The Green Man. Gail E. Haley. Ill. by the author. Scribner. 32 pp. (1981).
Grizzly Bear. Berniece Freschet. Ill. by Donald Carrick. Scribner. 40 pp. (1975).
Guess Who My Favorite Person Is. Byrd Baylor. Ill. by Robert Andrew Parker. Scribner. 32 pp. (1978).
Half a Kingdom. Ann McGovern. Ill. by Nola Langner. Warne. 38 pp. (1978). P, Scholastic.
Hamburgers—and Ice Cream for Dessert. Eleanor Clymer. Ill. by Roy Doty. Dutton. 48 pp. (1975).
Handmade Secret Hiding Places. Nonny Hogrogian. Ill. by the author. Overlook Press. 40 pp. (1975).
The Hand-Me-Down Kid. Francine Pascal. Viking. 172 pp. (1981).
Harriet and the Runaway Book. Johanna Johnston. Ill. by Ronald Himler. Harper. 80 pp. (1978).
Helga's Dowry: A Troll Love Story. Tomie de Paola. Ill by the author. Harcourt. 32 pp. (1978). P, Harcourt.
Henry Aaron: Sports Hero. Marshall and Sue Burchard. Ill. with photographs. Putnam. 96 pp. (1974).
The Hocus-Pocus Dilemma. Pat Kibbe. Ill. by Dan Jones. Knopf. 124 pp. (1980). P, Scholastic.
Horatio's Birthday. Eleanor Clymer. Ill. by Robert Quackenbush. Atheneum. 60 pp. (1977).
The House on Pendleton Block. Ann Waldron. Ill. by Sonia O. Lisker. Hastings. 151 pp. (1975).
The Housekeeper's Dog. Jerry Smith. Ill. by the author. Parents. 48 pp. (1981).
How Lazy Can You Get? Phyllis Reynolds Naylor. Ill. by Alan Daniel. Atheneum. 64 pp. (1980).

Hut School and the Wartime Homefront Heroes. Robert Burch. Ill. by Ronald
    Himler. Viking. 138 pp. (1974).
The I Hate Mathematics! Book. Marilyn Burns. Ill. by Martha Hairston. Little,
    Brown. 127 pp. (1975). P, Little, Brown.
I, Heracles. Elizabeth Silverthorne. Ill. by Billie Jean Osborne. Abindon.
    128 pp. (1979).
In the Circle of Time. Margaret J. Anderson. Knopf. 182 pp. (1980). P, Scholas-
    tic.
Is There an Actor in the House? Virginia Bradley. Dodd, Mead. 298 pp. (1975).
It's Not Fair. Charlotte Zolotow. Ill. by William Pene du Bois. Harper. 32 pp.
    (1977).
James Weldon Johnson. Ophelia Settle Egypt. Ill. by Moneta Barnett. Crowell.
    48 pp. (1974).
Jane, Wishing. Tobi Tobias. Ill. by Trina Schart Hyman. Viking. 48 pp. (1978).
Jinx Glove. Matt Christopher. Ill. by Norm Chartier. Little, Brown. 48 pp.
    (1974).
The Juice: Football's Superstar O.J. Simpson. Dick Belsky. Walck. 58 pp.
    (1978). O/P.
Kickle Snifters and Other Fearsome Critters. Alvin Schwartz. Ill. by Glen
    Rounds. Lippincott. 64 pp. (1977). P, Bantam.
Knock Knock: The Most Ever. William Cole. Ill. by Mike Thaler. Watts. 96 pp.
    (1977). O/P.
The Land Where Ice Cream Grows. Anthony Burgess. Ill. by Fulvio Testa.
    Doubleday. 32 pp. (1980).
Langston Hughes: American Poet. Alice Walker. Ill. by Don Miller. Crowell.
    40 pp. (1974).
Latki and the Lightning Lizard. Betty Baker. Ill. by Donald Carrick. Macmil-
    lan. 52 pp. (1980).
Left-Handed Shortstop. Patricia Reilly Giff. Ill. by Leslie Morrill. Delacorte.
    128 pp. (1981). P, Dell.
Leprechauns Never Lie. Lorna Balian. Ill. by the author. Abingdon. 32 pp.
    (1981).
Let's Make a Deal. Linda Glovach. Ill. by the author. Prentice. 48 pp. (1975).
The Lion in the Box. Marguerite de Angeli. Ill. by the author. Doubleday. 64 pp.
    (1975).
Lizzie Lies a Lot. Elizabeth Levy. Ill. by John Wallner. Delacorte. 102 pp.
    (1977). P, Dell.
Maggie Marmelstein for President. Marjorie Weinman Sharmat. Ill. by Ben
    Shecter. Harper. 128 pp. (1975). P, Harper.
The Magic Cooking Pot. Faith M. Towle. Ill. by the author. Houghton. 40 pp.
    (1975).
Make a Circle Keep Us In: Poems for a Good Day. Arnold Adoff. Ill. by Ronald
    Himler. Delacorte. 26 pp. (1975).
The Mariah Delaney Lending Library Disaster. Sheila Greenwald. Ill. by the
    author. Houghton. 123 pp. (1978).
Maria's House. Jean Merrill. Ill. by Frances Gruse Scott. Atheneum. 59 pp.
    (1974).
Mary McLeod Bethune. Eloise Greenfield. Ill. by Jerry Pinkney. Crowell. 32 pp.
    (1978).
McBroom Tells a Lie. Sid Fleischman. Ill. by Walter Lorraine. Atlantic-Little,
    Brown. 48 pp. (1977).
Me and the Terrible Two. Ellen Conford. Ill. by Charles Carroll. Little, Brown.
    121 pp. (1974). P, Pocket.
Meet the Vampire. Georgess McHargue. Ill. with drawings and photographs.
    Lippincott. 80 pp. (1980). P, Dell.

Merry Merry FIBruary. Doris Orgel. Ill. by Arnold Lobel. Parents. 28 pp. (1978).

Mice on Ice. Jane Yolen. Ill. by Lawrence DiFiori. Dutton. 72 pp. (1981).

Mice on My Mind. Bernard Waber. Ill. by the author. Houghton. 48 pp. (1978).

Mirror of Danger. Pamela Sykes. Lodestar/Dutton. 175 pp. (1974). P, Pocket.

Miss Nelson Is Missing. Harry Allard. Ill. by James Marshall. Houghton. 32 pp. (1978). P, Scholastic.

Moose, Goose, and Little Nobody. Ellen Raskin. Ill. by the author. Parents. 32 pp. (1974).

More Fables of Aesop. Retold by Jack Kent. Ill. by the author. Parents. 56 pp. (1974).

More Science Experiments You Can Eat. Vicki Cobb. Ill. by Giulio Maestro. Lippincott. 126 pp. (1980). P, Harper.

The Most Delicious Camping Trip Ever. Alice Bach. Ill. by Steven Kellogg. Harper. 46 pp. (1977). P, Dell.

Mouse and Tim. Faith McNulty. Ill. by Marc Simont. Harper. 48 pp. (1979).

Movie Monsters. Thomas Aylesworth. Ill. with photographs. Lippincott. 80 pp. (1975). P, Harper.

Mr. Mysterious's Secrets of Magic. Sid Fleischman. Ill. by Eric von Schmidt. Atlantic-Little, Brown. 81 pp. (1975).

Ms. Glee Was Waiting. Donna Hill. Ill. by Diane Dawson. Atheneum. 29 pp. (1979).

Muhammed Ali. Beth Wilson. Ill. by Floyd Sowell. Putnam. 64 pp. (1974). O/P.

Mummies Made in Egypt. Aliki. Ill. by the author. Crowell. 32 pp. (1980).

My Animals. William Armstrong. Ill. by Mirko Hanak. Doubleday. 32 pp. (1974). O/P.

My Daddy is a Cool Dude. Karama Fufuka. Ill. by Mahiri Fufuka. Dial. 40 pp. (1975).

My Grandson Lew. Charlotte Zolotow. Ill. by William Pene du Bois. Harper. 131 pp. (1974).

Near the Window Tree: Poems and Notes. Karla Kuskin. Ill. by the author. Harper. 64 pp. (1975).

Never Tickle a Turtle! Mike Thaler. Ill. by the author. Watts. 96 pp. (1978). P, Avon.

New Life: New Room. June Jordan. Ill. by Ray Cruz. Crowell. 53 pp. (1975).

No Arm in Left Field. Matt Christopher. Ill. by Byron Goto. Little, Brown. 135 pp. (1974).

Nonna. Jennifer Bartoli. Ill. by Joan E. Drescher. Harvey House. 48 pp. (1975).

North American Legends. Selected by Virginia Haviland. Ill. by Ann Strugnell. Philomel. 214 pp. (1980).

The Old Joke Book. Janet Ahlberg and Allan Ahlberg. Ill. by the authors. Viking. 30 pp. (1978). P, Puffin.

Old Mother Witch. Carol Carrick. Ill by Donald Carrick. Seabury. 32 pp. (1975).

The Old Woman and the Red Pumpkin. Betsy Bang. Ill. by Molly Garrett Bang. Macmillan. 32 pp. (1975).

Oliver Hyde's Dishcloth Concert. Richard Kennedy. Ill. by Robert Andrew Parker. Atlantic-Little, Brown. 47 pp. (1978).

An Orphan for Nebraska. Charlene Joy Talbot. Atheneum. 216 pp. (1980).

Owl at Home. Arnold Lobel. Ill. by the author. Harper. 64 pp. (1975).

The Pack Rat's Day and Other Poems. Jack Prelutsky. Ill. by Margaret Bloy Graham. Macmillan. 31 pp. (1974).

The Painter's Trick. Piero Ventura and Marisa Ventura. Ill. by the authors. Random. 34 pp. (1978).

Periwinkle. Roger Duvoisin. Ill. by the author. Knopf. 28 pp. (1977).

Pets in a Jar. Seymour Simon. Ill. by Betty Fraser. Viking. 96 pp. (1975). P, Puffin.
The Princess and Froggie. Harve Zemach and Kaethe Zemach. Ill. by Margot Zemach. Farrar. 46 pp. (1975).
The Queen and Rosie Randall. Helen Oxenbury (from an idea by Jill Buttfield-Campbell). Ill. by the author. Morrow. 40 pp. (1980).
The Quicksand Book. Tomie de Paola. Ill. by the author. Holiday. 32 pp. (1978).
The Rainbow-Colored Horse. Pura Belpré. Ill. by Antonio Martorell. Warne. 44 pp. (1979).
Ramona and Her Father. Beverly Cleary. Ill. by Alan Tiegreen. Morrow. (1978). P, Dell.
Ramona and Her Mother. Beverly Cleary. Ill. by Allan Tiegreen. Morrow. 208 pp. (1980). P, Dell.
Ramona the Brave. Beverly Cleary. Ill. by Allan Tiegreen. Morrow. 192 pp. (1975). P, Dell.
The Rascals from Haskell's Gym. Frank Bonham. Dutton. 119 pp. (1978). P, Scholastic.
The Return of the Great Brain. John D. Fitzgerald. Ill. by Mercer Mayer. Dial. 157 pp. (1974). P, Dell.
Roberto Clemente. Kenneth Rudeen. Ill. by Frank Mullins. Crowell. 40 pp. (1974).
The Robot and Rebecca: The Mystery of the Code-Carrying Kids. Jane Yolen. Ill. by Jurg Obrist. Knopf. 128 pp. (1981). P, Knopf.
Rosie's Double Dare. Robie H. Harris. Ill. by Tony De Luna. Knopf. 128 pp. (1981). P, Knopf.
Samantha on Stage. Susan Clement. Farrar. Ill. by Ruth Sanderson. Dial. 164 pp. (1980). P, Scholastic.
Sandy and the Rock Star. Walt Morey. Dutton. 190 pp. (1980). P, Scholastic.
Save the Earth: An Ecology Handbook. Betty Miles. Ill. by Claire A. Nivola. Knopf. 95 pp. (1974).
Sea Star. Robert M. McClung. Ill. by the author. Morrow. 48 pp. (1975).
Secrets. Nancy J. Hopper. Lodestar/Dutton. 138 pp. (1980).
Seeing Things: A Book of Poems. Robert Froman. Letterings by Ray Barber. Crowell. 59 pp. (1974).
Seven Spells to Sunday. Andre Norton and Phyllis Miller. McElderry/Atheneum. 144 pp. (1980). P, Pocket.
The 17 Gerbils of Class 4A. William H. Hooks. Ill. by Joel Schick. Coward. 56 pp. (1977).
The Sick of Being Sick Book. Jovial Bob Stine and Jane Stine. Ill. by Carol Nicklaus. Dutton. 80 pp. (1981).
The Sisters Impossible. James David Landis. Knopf. 174 pp. (1980). P, Bantam.
The Sleeping Beauty. Retold by Trina Schart Hyman. Ill. by the author. Little, Brown. 43 pp. (1978).
Small in the Saddle. Mark Allan Stamaty. Ill. by the author. Windmill. 32 pp. (1975). O/P.
Somebody Else's Child. Roberta Silman. Ill. by Chris Conover. Warne. 64 pp. (1977).
Something Queer on Vacation. Elizabeth Levy. Ill. by Mordicai Gerstein. Delacorte. 48 pp. (1981).
Soonie and the Dragon. Shirley Rousseau Murphy. Ill. by Susan Vaeth. Atheneum. 96 pp. (1980).
The Sorcerer's Apprentice. Wanda Gag. Ill. by Margot Tomes. Coward. 32 pp. (1980).

Sports Hero: O.J. Simpson. Marshall Burchard. Ill. with photographs. Putnam. 96 pp. (1975).

The Star Child. Oscar Wilde. Ill. by Fiona French. Four Winds. 32 pp. (1980).

Strega Nona. Tomie de Paola. Ill. by the author. Prentice. 32 pp. (1975). P, Prentice.

Summer of the Stallion. June Andrea Hanson. Ill. by Gloria Singer. Macmillan. 108 pp. (1980).

Sums: A Looking Game. Diane Vreuls. Viking. 48 pp. (1978).

Superfudge. Judy Blume. Dutton. 166 pp. (1981). P, Dell.

Taxi Dog. Svend Otto. Ill. by the author. Four Winds. 29 pp. (1979).

The Terrible Thing that Happened at Our House. Marge Blaine. Ill. by John C. Wallner. Parents. 40 pp. (1975).

They Put on Masks. Byrd Baylor. Ill. by Jerry Ingram. Scribner. 48 pp. (1974).

Things Won't Be the Same. Kathryn Ewing. Harcourt. 96 pp. (1981).

Thirteen. Remy Charlip and Jerry Joyner. Ill. by the authors. Four Winds. 28 pp. (1975).

Thor Heyerdahl and the Reed Boat Ra. Barbara Beasley Murphy and Norman Baker. Ill. with photographs. Lippincott. 64 pp. (1974).

Thumbelina. Hans Christian Andersen. Retold by Amy Ehrlich. Ill. by Susan Jeffers. Dial. 32 pp. (1980).

A Time to Keep Silent. Gloria Whelan. Putnam. 128 pp. (1980).

Top Secret: Alligator! Harold Goodwin. Ill. by the author. Bradbury. 95 pp. (1975). P, Dell.

Tracy Austin. Nancy Robison. Ill. with photographs. Harvey. 60 pp. (1979).

The Trouble with Thirteen. Betty Miles. Knopf. 108 pp. (1980). P, Avon.

The Upside-Down Man. Russell Baker. Ill. by Gahan Wilson. McGraw. 48 pp. (1978).

A Very Young Gymnast. Jill Krementz. Ill. with photographs by the author. Knopf. 125 pp. (1979).

A Very Young Rider. Jill Krementz. Photographs by the author. Knopf. 119 pp. (1978).

Warton and Morton. Russell E. Erickson. Ill. by Lawrence Di Fiori. Lothrop. 64 pp. (1977). P, Dell.

The Well-Mannered Balloon. Nancy Willard. Ill. by Haig and Regina Shekerjian. Harcourt. 28 pp. (1977).

What Can She Be? An Architect. Gloria Goldreich and Esther Goldreich. Photographs by Robert Ipcar. Lothrop. 46 pp. (1974).

What's the Big Idea, Ben Franklin? Jean Fritz. Ill. by Margot Tomes. Coward. 48 pp. (1977). P, Coward.

When Lucy Went Away. G. Max Ross. Ill. by Ingrid Fetz. Dutton. 26 pp. (1977).

Where Are You, Angela von Hauptmann, Now That I Need You? Barbara Williams. Holt. 192 pp. (1980).

Whoppers: Tall Tales and Other Lies. Alvin Schwartz. Ill. by Glen Rounds. Lippincott. 128 pp. (1975). P, Lippincott.

Why Noah Chose the Dove. Isaac Bashevis Singer. Ill. by Eric Carle. Farrar. 28 pp. (1974).

Will You Sign Here, John Hancock? Jean Fritz. Ill. by Trina Schart Hyman. Coward. 47 pp. (1977). P, Coward.

The Wish at the Top. Clyde Robert Bulla. Ill. by Chris Conover. Crowell. 32 pp. (1974).

Words by Heart. Ouida Sebestyen. Atlantic-Little, Brown. 162 pp. (1980). P, Bantam.

The Worst Witch. Jill Murphy. Ill. by the author. Allison and Busby. 72 pp. (1981).

Zag: A Search through the Alphabet. Robert Tallon. Ill. by the author. Holt. 64 pp. (1977). O/P.

Older Readers

Absolute Zero. Helen Cresswell. Macmillan. 174 pp. (1979). P, Avon.

Accident. Hila Colman. Morrow. 192 pp. (1981). P, Pocket.

Alan and the Animal Kingdom. Isabelle Holland. Lippincott. 192 pp. (1978).

Alan Mendelsohn, The Boy from Mars. Daniel M. Pinkwater. Dutton. 240 pp. (1980). P, Bantam.

Alvin's Swap Shop. Clifford B. Hicks. Ill. by Bill Sokol. Holt. 143 pp. (1977). P, Scholastic.

Bagthorpes Unlimited. Helen Cresswell. Macmillan. 180 pp. (1977).

Bargain Bride. Evelyn Sibley Lampman. McElderry/Atheneum. 180 pp. (1978). P, Atheneum.

The Baron's Hostage. Geoffrey Trease. Lodestar/Dutton. 160 pp. (1975). O/P.

Beauty and the Beast. Retold by Marianna Mayer. Ill. by Mercer Mayer. Four Winds. 44 pp. (1979).

Ben and Annie. Joan Tate. Ill. by Judith Gwyn Brown. Doubleday. 80 pp. (1978). O/P.

A Billion for Boris. Mary Rodgers. Harper. 216 pp. (1974). P, Harper.

Blubber. Judy Blume. Bradbury. 158 pp. (1974). P, Dell.

Blue Fin. Colin Thiele. Harper. 248 pp. (1974). P, Harper.

The Borrowed House. Hilda van Stockum. Farrar. 215 pp. (1975).

Bright Sunset: The Story of an Indian Girl. Ruth Wheeler. Ill. by Dorothy Matteson. Lothrop. 127 pp. (1974). O/P.

Bruno. Achim Broger. Ill. by Ronald Himler. Morrow. 160 pp. (1975).

Can You Sue Your Parents for Malpractice? Paula Danziger. Delacorte. 152 pp. (1980). P, Dell.

The Case of the Baker Street Irregular. Robert Newman. Atheneum. 216 pp. (1979). P, Bantam.

The Code & Cipher Book. Jane Sarnoff and Reynold Ruffins. Ill. by Reynold Ruffins. Scribner. 40 pp. (1975). P, Scribner.

Connie. Anne Alexander. Ill. by Gail Owens. Atheneum. 179 pp. (1977).

Cute is a Four-Letter Word. Stella Pevsner. Clarion/Houghton. 190 pp. (1981). P, Pocket.

A Dance to Still Music. Barbara Corcoran. Ill. by Charles Robinson. Atheneum. 184 pp. (1974). P, Atheneum.

The Dark Didn't Catch Me. Crystal Thrasher. Atheneum/McElderry. 182 pp. (1975). P, Atheneum.

Deborah Sampson: Soldier of the Revolution. Harold W. Felton. Ill. by John Martinez. Dodd. 111 pp. (1977).

The Devil's Storybook. Natalie Babbitt. Ill. by the author. Farrar. 105 pp. (1974).

Does Anybody Care about Lou Emma Miller? Alberta Wilson Constant. Crowell. 278 pp. (1980).

Dogsbody. Diana Wynne Jones. Greenwillow. 242 pp. (1978).

Dorrie's Book. Marilyn Sachs. Ill. by Anne Sachs. Doubleday. 144 pp. (1975).

Dr. Elizabeth: A Biography of the First Woman Doctor. Patricia Clapp. Lothrop. 155 pp. (1974). O/P.

Dragonwings. Laurence Yep. Harper. 248 pp. (1975). P, Harper.

The Face at the Window. Wolfgang Ecke. Trans. from the German by Stella Humphries and Vernon Humphries. Ill. by Rolf Rettich. Prentice. 134 pp. (1981).

Fast Sam, Coole Clyde and Stuff. Walter Dean Myers. Viking. 190 pp. (1975). P, Avon.

Father's Arcane Daughter. E.L. Konigsburg. Atheneum. 118 pp. (1977). P, Atheneum.

The Figure in the Shadows. John Bellairs. Ill. by Mercer Mayer. Dial. 155 pp. (1975). P, Dell.

Foster Child. Marion Dane Bauer. Clarion/Houghton. 155 pp. (1978). P, Dell.

Fridays. Patricia Lee Gauch. Putnam. 160 pp. (1980). P, Pocket.

From Prison to the Major Leagues: The Picture Story of Ron LeFlore. Ron Knapp. Ill. with photographs. Messner. 64 pp. (1981).

Frozen Fire. James Houston. McElderry/Atheneum. 149 pp. (1978). P. Atheneum.

The Ghost Belonged to Me. Richard Peck. Viking. 183 pp. (1975). P, Avon.

Ghost I Have Been. Richard Peck. Viking. 214 pp. (1978). P, Dell.

The Giant Book of Strange but True Sports Stories. Howard Liss. Ill. by Joe Mathieu. Random. 147 pp. (1977).

The Girl Who Had No Name. Berniece Rabe. Dutton. 149 pp. (1978).

The Girl Who Lived on the Ferris Wheel. Louise Moeri. Dutton. 118 pp. (1980). P, Avon.

The Glad Man. Gloria Gonzalez. Knopf. 160 pp. (1975).

Going Back. Penelope Lively. Dutton. 128 pp. (1975) O/P.

Good-By to Stony Crick. Kathryn Borland and Helen Speicher. Ill. by Deanne Hollinger. McGraw-Hill. 138 pp. (1975). O/P.

Greenwitch. Susan Cooper. McElderry/Atheneum. 153 pp. (1974). P, Atheneum.

Hangin' Out with Cici. Fracine Pascal. Viking. 152 pp. (1978). P, Pocket.

Haunted. Judith St. George. Putnam. 160 pp. (1981).

The Haunting of Julie Unger. Valerie A. Lutters. Atheneum. 193 pp. (1978).

The Headless Roommate and Other Tales of Terror. Daniel Cohen. Ill. by Peggy Brier. Evans. 128 pp. (1981).

How I Came to Be a Writer. Phyllis Reynolds Naylor. Ill. with memorabilia. Atheneum. 133 pp. (1979).

How to Eat Fried Worms and Other Plays. Thomas Rockwell. Ill. by Joel Schick. Delacorte. 144 pp. (1981). P, Dell.

In Our House Scott Is My Brother. C.S. Adler. Macmillan. 144 pp. (1981).

The Innkeeper's Daughter. Barbara Cohen. Lothrop. 160 pp. (1980).

Into the Dream. William Sleator. Ill. by Ruth Sanderson. Dutton. 144 pp. (1980).

Into the Unknown: Nine Astounding Stories. Stephen Mooser. Ill. with photos, line drawings, and lithographs. Lippincott. 128 pp. (1981).

It Can't Hurt Forever. Marilyn Singer. Ill. by Leigh Grant. Harper. 192 pp. (1979). P, Harper.

Jaguar, My Twin. Betty Jean Lifton. Ill. by Ann Leggett. Atheneum. 114 pp. (1977).

Jokes to Read in the Dark. Scott Corbett. Ill. by Annie Gusman. Dutton/Unicorn. 80 pp. (1981). P, Dutton.

The Journey Back. Johanna Reiss. Crowell. 212 pp. (1977).

Journey Home. Hoshiko Uchida. Ill. by Charles Robinson. McElderry/Atheneum. 131 pp. (1979).

Just Between Us. Susan Beth Pfeffer. Ill. by Lorna Tomei. Delacorte. 120 pp. (1981). P, Dell.

Kate Alone. Patricia Lee Gauch. Putnam. 112 pp. (1981).

Konrad. Christine Nostlinger. Translated by Anthea Bell. Ill. by Carol Nicklaus. Watts. 135 pp. O/P.

Ladies of the Gothics: Tales of Romance and Terror by the Gentle Sex. Selected by Seon Manley and Gogo Lewis. Lothrop. 224 pp. (1975).

The Last Monster. Jane Annixter and Paul Annixter. Harcourt. 84 pp. (1981).

Laws and Trials that Created History. Brandt Aymar and Edward Sagarin. Crown. 222 pp. (1974).

The Lemon Meringue Dog. Walt Morey. Dutton. 176 pp. (1981).

The Letter, the Witch, and the Ring. John Bellairs. Ill. by Richard Egielski. Dial. 188 pp. (1977). P, Dell.

Like Everybody Else. Barbara Girion. Scribner. 176 pp. (1981).
The Lines Are Coming, A Book about Drawing. Hans-Georg Rauch. Ill. by the author. Scribner. 56 pp. (1979).
Lizard Music. D. Manus Pinkwater. Ill. by the author. Dodd. 157 pp. (1977).
Lori. Gloria Goldreich. Holt. 182 pp. (1980).
Love Is Like Peanuts. Betty Bates. Holiday. 128 pp. (1981).
The Luck of Brin's Five. Cherry Wilder. Atheneum. 230 pp. (1978).
The Magic of the Glits. C.S. Adler. Ill. by Ati Forberg. Macmillan. 132 pp. (1980).
Man from the Sky. Avi. Ill. by David Wiesner. Knopf. 120 pp. (1981).
The Man with the Silver Eyes. William O. Steele. Harcourt. 147 pp. (1977).
Masquerade. Kit Williams. Ill. by the author. Schocken. 32 pp. (1981).
Maudie and Me and the Dirty Book. Betty Miles. Knopf. 160 pp. (1981). P, Avon.
Merry Ever After: The Story of Two Medieval Weddings. Joe Lasker. Ill. by the author. Viking. 48 pp. (1977). P, Puffin.
Midnight Is a Place. Joan Aiken. Viking. 286 pp. (1974).
The Missing Persons League. Frank Bonham. Dutton. 157 pp. (1977). P, Scholastic.
Modern Football Superstars. Bill Gutman. Ill. with photographs. Dodd. 127 pp. (1974).
Mr. McFadden's Hallowe'en. Rumer Godden. Viking. 127 pp. (1975). O/P.
My Black Me: A Beginning Book of Black Poetry. Arnold Adoff, Ed. Dutton. 95 pp. (1974).
My Brother, the Thief. Marlene Fanta Shyer. Scribner. 138 pp. (1981).
The Night Swimmers. Betsy Byars. Delacorte. 144 pp. (1981). P, Dell.
Nightmare Town. T. Ernesto Bethancourt. Holiday. 158 pp. (1980).
Only Love. Susan Sallis. Harper. 256 pp. (1981). P, Dell.
Philip Hall Likes Me. I Reckon Maybe. Bette Green. Ill. by Charles Lilly. Dial. 141 pp. (1974). P, Dell.
The Pinballs. Betsy Byars. Harper. 136 pp. (1978). P, Scholastic.
The Pistachio Prescription. Paula Danziger. Delacorte. 160 pp. (1979). P, Dell.
A Present for Yanya. Peggy Mann and Katica Prusina. Ill. by Douglas Gorsline. Random. 119 pp. (1975).
Refugee. Anne Ross. Dial. 118 pp. (1978).
A Ring of Endless Light. Madeleine L'Engle. Farrar. 356 pp. (1981). P, Dell.
Robbers, Bones, and Mean Dogs. Compiled by Barry and Velma Berkey. Ill. by Marylin Hafner. Addison. 25 pp. (1979).
Rosie and Michael. Judith Viorst. Ill. by Lorna Tomei. Atheneum. 40 pp. (1974). P, Atheneum.
Runaway to Freedom: A Story of the Underground Railway. Barbara Smucker. Ill. by Charles Lilly. Harper. 160 pp. (1979). P, Harper.
The Saving of P.S. Robbie Branscum. Ill. by Glen Rounds. Doubleday. 127 pp. (1978). P, Dell.
A Second Springtime. Gordon Cooper. Lodestar/Dutton. 223 pp. (1975). O/P.
Secret Lives. Berthe Amoss. Atlantic-Little, Brown. 192 pp. (1980). P, Dell.
Showboat in the Backcourt. William Campbell Gault. Dutton. 122 pp. (1977).
Sideways Stories from Wayside School. Louis Sachar. Ill. by Dennis Hockerman. Follett. 139 pp. (1979).
The Solid Gold Kid. Norma Fox Mazer and Harry Mazer. Delacorte. 219 pp. (1978). P, Dell.
Someone Slightly Different. Judy Frank Mearian. Dial. 192 pp. (1981).
The Story of American Photography. Martin W. Sandler. Ill. with photographs. Little, Brown. 318 pp. (1980).
Street Gangs, Yesterday and Today. James Haskins. Ill. with prints and photographs. Hastings. 154 pp. (1974). P, Hastings.

A Summer to Die. Lois Lowry. Ill. by Jenni Oliver. Houghton. 154 pp. (1978). P, Bantam.

Superstars of the Sports World. Bill Gutman. Ill. with photographs. Messner. 96 pp. (1979).

A Swiftly Tilting Planet. Madeleine L'Engle. Farrar. 278 pp. (1979). P, Dell.

The Swing. Emily Hanlon. Bradbury. 210 pp. (1980). P, Dell.

Tawn. Chas Carner. Ill. by Donald Carrick. Macmillan. 160 pp. (1979).

Teetoncey and Ben O'Neal. Theodore Taylor. Ill. by Richard Cuffari. Doubleday. 184 pp. (1975). P, Avon.

There Are Two Kinds of Terrible. Peggy Mann. Doubleday. 132 pp. (1980). P, Avon.

There's a Bat in Bunk Five. Paula Danziger. Delacorte. 150 pp. (1981). P, Dell.

The Tiger's Bones and Other Plays for Children. Ted Hughes. Ill. by Alan E. Cober. Viking. 141 pp. (1974).

The Transfigured Hart. Jane Yolen. Ill. by Donna Diamond. Crowell. 86 pp. (1975).

Trial Valley. Vera Cleaver and Bill Cleaver. Lippincott. 158 pp. (1978). P, Bantam.

Tuck Everlasting. Natalie Babbitt. Farrar. 139 pp. (1975). P, Bantam.

The Turning Place. Jean E. Karl. Dutton. 213 pp. (1977). P, Dell.

The Way It Was—1876. Suzanne Hilton. Ill. with old prints and photographs. Westminster. 216 pp. (1975).

The Way Things Are and Other Poems. Myra Cohn Livingston. Ill. by Jenni Oliver. McElderry/Atheneum. 45 pp. (1974).

We Interrupt This Semester for a Very Important Bulletin. Ellen Conford. Little, Brown. 176 pp. (1980).

Weakfoot. Linda Cline. Lothrop 160 pp. (1975). O/P.

What If They Knew? Patricia Hermes. Harcourt. 132 pp. (1981). P, Dell.

What's the Matter with the Dobsons? Hila Colman. Crown. 120 pp. (1981). P, Pocket.

Whistle in the Graveyard: Folktales to Chill Your Bones. Maria Leach. Ill. by ken Rinciari. Viking. 131 pp. (1974).

Who Stole Kathy Young? Margaret Goff Clark. Dodd. 192 pp. (1981).

The Whole Mirth Catalog. Michael Scheier and Julie Frankel. Ill. by the authors. Watts. 96 pp. (1979). P, Watts.

Wildfire. Mavis Thorpe Clark. Macmillan. 219 pp. (1974).

The Winds of Time. Barbara Corcoran. Ill. by Gail Owens. Atheneum. 169 pp. (1974).

Winter Wheat. Jeanne Williams. Putnam. 157 pp. (1975). O/P.

With a Wave of the Wand. Mark Jonathan Harris. Lothrop. 192 pp. (1981).

Wonder Wheels. Lee Bennett Hopkins. Knopf. 172 pp. (1980). P, Dell.

Your Old Pal, Al. Constance C. Green. Viking. 156 pp. (198). P, Dell.

Informational Books

Barn Owl. Phyllis Flower. Ill. by Cherryl Pape. Harper. 62 pp. (1979).

Basketball Players Do Amazing Things. Mel Cebalash. Random. 69 pp. (1977).

Bear's Heart. Burton Supree with Ann Ross. Ill. by Bear's Heart. Lippincott. 63 pp. (1978).

Bees Can't Fly, But They Do. David C. Knight. Ill. by Barbara Wolff. Macmillan. 48 pp. (1977).

Brothers Are All the Same. Mary Milgram. Photographs by Rosmarie Hausherr. Dutton. 32 pp. (1979).

Can't You Make Them Behave, King George? Jean Fritz. Ill. by Tomie de Paola. Coward. 48 pp. (1978). P, Coward.

Catfish Hunter: The Three Million Dollar Arm. Irwin Stambler. Putnam. 128 pp. (1977).

A Chick Hatches. Joanna Cole. Photographs by Jerome Wexler. Morrow. 47 pp. (1977).

A Cricket in the Grass. Philip Van Soelen. Ill. by the author. Sierra Club/Scribner. 128 pp. (1980).

Dinosaur Days. David C. Knight. Ill. by Joel Schick. McGraw. 48 pp. (1978).

Dollhouse Magic: How to Make and Find Simple Dollhouse Furniture. P.K. Roche. Photographs by John Knott. Ill. by Richard Cuffari. Dial. 56 pp. (1978). P, Dial.

Dorothy Hamill Olympic Champion. Elizabeth Van Steenurpk. Photographs by David Leonardi. Harvey. 56 pp. (1977).

Dragons and Other Fabulous Beasts. Richard Blythe. Ill. by Fiona French and Joanna Troughton. Grosset. 64 pp. (1981).

The Easy Hockey Book. Jonah Kalb. Ill. by Bill Morrison. Houghton. 64 pp. (1978).

Fiddle with a Riddle. Joanne E. Berenstein. Ill. by Giulio Maestro. Dutton. 72 pp. (1980).

Good for Me! All About Food in 32 Bites. Marilyn Burns. Ill. by Sandy Clifford. Little, Brown. 128 pp. (1979). P, Little, Brown.

Great Unsolved Cases. Arnold Madison. Ill. by Michael Deas. Watts. 88 pp. (1979). P, Dell.

Halloween. Joyce K. Kessel. Ill. by Nancy L. Carlson. Carolrhoda. 48 pp. (1981).

Here a Ghost, There a Ghost. Elizabeth P. Hoffman. Ill. by David kingham. Messner. 96 pp. (1979).

How to Turn Lemons into Money. Louise Armstrong. Ill. by Bill Basso. Harcourt. 28 pp. (1977). P, Harcourt.

I Have a Sister—My Sister is Deaf. Jeanne Whitehouse Peterson. Ill. by Deborah Ray. Harper. 32 pp. (1978).

Ink, Art, and All That. Vernon Pizer. Ill. by Tom Huffman. Putnam. 122 pp. (1977).

Jacques Cousteau. Genie Iverson. Ill. by Hal. Ashmead. Putnam. 63 pp. (1977).

Jambo Means Hello: Swahili Alphabet Book. Muriel Feelings. Ill. by Tom Feelings. Dial. 60 pp. (1974). P, Dial.

Kid Camping from AAAAIII! To Zip. Patrick F. McManus. Ill. by Roy Doty. Lothrop. 125 pp. (1980).

The Little Deer of the Florida Keys. Hope Ryden. Ill. with photographs by the author. Putnam. 64 pp. (1979).

Made in America: Eight Great All-American Creations. Murray Suid and Ron Harris. Ill. with photographs. Addison. 192 pp. (1979). P, Addison.

The Making of a Detective. Robert H. Millimaki. Lippincott. 94 pp. (1977).

Model Buildings and How to Make Them. Harvey Weiss. Ill. with photographs and drawings by the author. Crowell. 96 pp. (1980).

Motorcycle Moto Cross School. Ed and Dan Radlauer. Ill. with photographs by the authors. Watts. 44 pp. (1975).

Movie Stunts and the People Who Do Them. Gloria D. Miklowitz. Ill. with photographs. Harcourt. 64 pp. (1981). P, Harcourt.

Muhammed Ali. Kenneth Rudeen. Ill. by George Ford. Crowell. 34 pp. (1977).

My Brother Steven Is Retarded. Langsam Sobol. Photographs by Patricia Agre. Macmillan. 26 pp. (1978).

A Nest of Wood Ducks. Evelyn Shaw. Ill. by Cherryl Pape. Harper. 62 pp. (1977).

Ocean Frontiers. Eryl Davies. Ill. with photographs and diagrams. Viking. 64 pp. (1981).

Octopus. Carol Carrick. Ill. by Donald Carrick. Clarion/Houghton. 32 pp. (1979).

100 Greatest Women in Sports. Phyllis Hollander. Grosset. 142 pp. (1977). O/P.
Patriots in Petticoats. Patricia Edwards Clyne. Ill. by Richard Lebenson. Dodd. 144 pp. (1977).
Popcorn. Millicent Selsam. Photographs by Jerome Wexler. Morrow. 48 pp. (1977).
The Popcorn Book. Tomie de Paola. Ill. by the author. Holiday. 32 pp. (1979). P, Scholastic.
Pyramid. David Macaulay. Ill. by the author. Houghton. 80 pp. (1975). P, Houghton.
Roman Numerals. David Adler. Ill. by Byron Barton. Crowell. 33 pp. (1978).
Sand Tiger Shark. Carol Carrick. Ill. by Donald Carrick. Seabury. 28 pp. (1978).
The Sea World Book of Sharks. Eve Bunting. Ill. with photographs by Flip Nicklin. Harcourt. 80 pp. (1981).
The Skateboard Book. Ben Davidson. Grossett. 105 pp. (1977). O/P.
Skateboards: How to Make Them, How to Ride Them. Glenn Bunting and Eve Bunting. Harvey. 39 pp. (1978). P, Scholastic.
Small Habitats. Lilo Hess. Photographs by the author. Scribner. 49 pp. (1977).
Small Worlds Close Up. Lisa Grillone and Joseph Gennaro. Ill. with photographs. Crown. 61 pp. (1979).
The Story of Nim: The Chimp Who Learned Language. Anna Michel. Ill. with photographs by Susan Kuklin and Herbert S. Terrace. Knopf. 60 pp. (1981).
The Story of Stevie Wonder. James Haskins. Lothrop. 126 pp. (1977).
The Story of Vampires. Thomas G. Aylesworth. McGraw. 85 pp. (1978).
Take Me Out to the Airfield! How the Wright Brothers Invented the Airplane. Robert Quackenbush. Parents. 31 pp. (1977). O/P.
Television Magic. Eurfron Gwynne Jones. Ill. with photographs and drawings. Viking. 62 pp. (1979).
Two Kittens Are Born. Betty Schilling. Ill. with photographs by the author. Holt. 44 pp. (1981).
Tyrannosaurus Rex. Millicent Selsam. Ill. with photographs. Harper. 38 pp. (1979).
Unbuilding. David Macaulay. Ill. by the author. Houghton. 80 pp. (1981).
Underground. David Macaulay. Ill. by the author. Houghton. 112 pp. (1977).
Weird and Wacky Inventions. Jim Murphy. Ill. by the author. Crown. 96 pp. (1979).
Wesley Paul, Marathon Runner. Julianna A. Foge. Photographs by Mary S. Watkins. Lippincott. 48 pp. (1980).
The Wild Inside. Linda Allison. Ill. by the author. Sierra Club/Scribner. 144 pp. (1980). P, Sierra Club.
The Wild Rabbit. Oxford Scientific Films. Ill. with photographs by George Bernard. Putnam. 32 pp. (1981).

Poetry/Verse

Alligator Pie. Dennie Lee. Ill. by Frank Newfield. Houghton. 64 pp. (1975).

The Baby's Lap Book. Compiled by Kay Chorao. Ill. by the author. Dutton. 64 pp. (1978).

The Bed Book. Sylvia Plath. Ill. by Emily Arnold McCully. Harper. 40 pp. (1977).

Best Wishes, Amen: A New Collection of Autograph Verse. Compiled by Lillian Morrison. Ill. by Loretta Lustig. Crowell. 208 pp. (1974).

Casey at the Bat. Ernest Lawrence Thayer. Ill. by Wallace Tripp. Coward. 32 pp. (1979). P, Coward.

A Child's Bestiary. John Garner. Ill. by Lucy, Joel, Joan, and John Gardner. Knopf. 69 pp. (1978).

The Gobble-Uns'll Git You Ef You Don't Watch Out! James Whitcomb Riley. Ill. by Joel Schick. Lippincott. 42 pp. (1975).

Granfa Grig Had a Pig and Other Rhymes Without Reason from Mother Goose. Compiled by Wallace Tripp. Ill. by the compiler. Little, Brown. 96 pp. (1977). P, Little, Brown.

A House Is a House For Me. Mary Ann Hoberman. Ill. by Betty Fraser. Viking. 48 pp. (1979).

Hurry, Hurry, Mary Dear! N.M. Bodecker. Atheneum/McElderry. 118 pp. (1977).

The Mean Old Mean Hyena. Jack Prelutsky. Ill. by Arnold Lobel. Greenwillow. 32 pp. (1979).

More Small Poems. Valerie Worth. Ill. by Natalie Babbitt. Farrar. 41 pp. (1977).

Nightmares: Poems to Trouble Your Sleep. Jack Prelutsky. Ill. by Arnold Lobel. Greenwillow. 38 pp. (1977).

See My Lovely Poison Ivy. Lilian Moore. Ill. by Diane Dawson. Atheneum. 42 pp. (1975).

Stopping by Woods on a Snowy Evening. Robert Frost. Ill. by Susan Jeffers. Dutton. 37 pp. (1979).

Tornado! Arnold Adoff. Ill. by Ronald Himler. Delacorte. 44 pp. (1978).

Wind, Sand, and Sky. Rebecca Caudill. Ill. by Donald Carrick. Dutton. 27 pp. (1977).

Witch Poems. Edited by Daisy Wallace. Ill. by Trina Schart Hyman. Holiday. 32 pp. (1977).

With a Deep Sea Smile: Story Hour Stretches for Large or Small Groups. Selected by Virginia A. Tashjian. Ill. by Rosemary Wells. Little, Brown. 140 pp. (1974).

Other *Books Published By* ira